话长城

迹／长／城／的／故／事

以随笔的形式记录张家口长城的风姿

王立军 著

辽宁美术出版社
LIAONING FINE ARTS PUBLISHING HOUSE

图书在版编目（CIP）数据

绘话长城/郭志红，王立军著 . — 沈阳：辽宁美术出版社，2024.4
ISBN 978-7-5314-9187-3

Ⅰ.①绘… Ⅱ.①郭… ②王… Ⅲ.长城—图集 Ⅳ.K928.77-64

中国版本图书馆CIP数据核字（2022）第001783号

出 版 者：	辽宁美术出版社
地 址：	沈阳市和平区民族北街29号　邮编：110001
发 行 者：	辽宁美术出版社
印 刷 者：	辽宁鼎籍数码科技有限公司
开 本：	889mm×1194mm　1/32
印 张：	6
字 数：	130千字
出版时间：	2024年4月第1版
印刷时间：	2024年4月第1次印刷
责任编辑：	严　赫
责任校对：	满　媛
装帧设计：	孙雨薇
英文翻译：	郭尚宜
书 号：	ISBN 978-7-5314-9187-3
定 价：	86.00元

邮购部电话：024-83833008
E-mail：lnmscbs@163.com
http://www.lnmscbs.cn
图书如有印装质量问题请与出版部联系调换
出版部电话：024-23835227

本书为河北省社会科学基金项目成果，项目批准号HB20YS055，项目名称"图解张家口长城建造样式"。

The book is supported by the Government of Hebei Province Social Science Foundation, with Project Approval Number HB20YS055, Project Name is "Illustrated Construction Style of the Zhangjiakou Great Wall".

绘话长城

序
Preface

序

长城是什么？是一个名词；是一篇文字；是一段历史更迭；是一项伟大工程；是一次战争；是一座城关；是犹如山川河流那样连绵不断的墙；是一块砖；是一堆沙土——无论是抽象的文字还是具象的图片，或者又是直观的体验。"长城"的样貌和意义在每个人心中有着不同的定位。如今，长城作为古代建筑物，其内质已经远远超出它原有的功能属性，长城的丰富表征和深厚意涵都值得我们去探寻。

万里长城万里长，长城脚下是家乡；万里长城永不倒，锦绣河山是怀抱。各种充满深情的讴歌久久回荡。旋律中徐徐展开一幅幅画卷，慢慢讲述长城的故事，本书以绘画和随笔的形式记录张家口长城的风姿。

What is the Great Wall? It is a noun and a text. It is a great project for historical change. It is a war and a city gate. It is also a continuous wall such as mountains and rivers, which are made from brick and piles of sand. Although it is an abstract word an actual picture, or even a visual experience.

Everyone has different perspectives on the appearance and the meaning of the "Great Wall". Nowadays the Great Wall as an ancient building, has a deeper internal meaning than its original functional attributes. The Great Wall is worth exploring the extensive-expression form and deep cultural heritage.

The Great Wall is thousands of miles long, and at the foot of the Great Wall is the hometown. The Great Wall will never collapse, and the splendid rivers and mountains embraced all around with deep enthusiastic songs echoing for a long time. Slowly unfolding multiple scrolls in the melody and telling the story of the Great Wall. This book records the beauty of Zhangjiakou's Great Wall in the form of paintings and essays.

目录
CONTENTS

■ 开篇小知识
The knowledge at the beginning

长城的名字　011
新中国的长城文化　012
张家口被誉为历代长城"博物馆"　014
长城的修建原则　016
以险制塞的空间原则　018
就地取材的施工原则　020
纵深防御的布局原则　022
长城纵深防御建构的原则　024
分段承包的施工原则　026
"物勒工名"　028
长城的构成形式　030
长城本体　032
附建在长城本体上的结构设施　034
障墙　036
其他相关建筑　038

■ 画卷徐徐展开
The scroll slowly unfolds

图1　赤城　046
图2　赤城长伸地堡长城　047
图3　赤城冰山梁长城　048
图4　赤城雕鹗土筑长城　049
图5　赤城独石口长城全景　050
图6　赤城独石口长城局部　051
图7　赤城独石口堡长城墙基局部　052
图8　赤城独石口堡西南侧墙体　053
图9　赤城独石口长城　054
图10　赤城海家窑长城　055
图11　赤城马连口长城　056

图12　赤城盘道界楼匾额　058
图13　赤城清泉堡北门　059
图14　赤城清泉堡北门侧面图　060
图15　赤城清泉堡南门敌楼匾额　062
图16　赤城县上堡村"新添镇川墩"　063
图17　赤城松树堡城门楼　064
图18　赤城长城　065
图19　赤城长沟门坝头长城　066
图20　赤城长伸地堡镇房楼匾额　067
图21　赤城长伸地堡镇房楼　068
图22　赤城长伸地堡旗杆基石　069
图23　赤城镇安堡长城　070
图24　崇礼　072
图25　赤城和崇礼交界的马连口长城局部　073
图26　赤城和崇礼交界的马连口长城全景　074
图27　崇礼清三营乡长城　076
图28　沽源　078
图29　沽源盘道沟长城　079
图30　沽源和赤城交界的长城　080
图31　怀安　081
图32　怀安渡口堡西门　082
图33　怀安马市口长城　084
图34　怀安桃平盘道门长城敌楼　085
图35　怀来　086
图36　怀来水头长城　087
图37　怀来水头长城圆形敌楼马面全景　088
图38　怀来陈家堡长城　090
图39　怀来陈家堡将军楼　092
图40　怀来陈家堡长城由双砖结构砌成　093
图41　怀来大营盘　094
图42　怀来鸡鸣山驿匾额　096
图43　怀来鸡鸣驿城墙　097
图44　怀来罗锅长城　098
图45　怀来罗锅长城箭孔　099
图46　怀来石洞3号敌台　100
图47　怀来水头长城　101
图48　怀来样边长城供士兵上下城墙的台阶　102
图49　怀来样边长城内侧每200米一个门洞，有台阶供上下　103
图50　怀来样边长城水门特写　104

图51	怀来样边长城水门样式　105
图52	康保　106
图53	康保金界壕1　107
图54	康保金界壕2　108
图55	尚义　109
图56	尚义地上村（西赵家窑）长城　110
图57	市区　111
图58	堡子里文昌阁　112
图59	桥东区威远台　114
图60	桥西区东窑子镇墩台　115
图61	市区石匠窑长城　116
图62	市区石匠窑至菜市村长城　117
图63	西镜门　118
图64	万全　119
图65	教堂楼两角度　120
图66	万全教堂楼　121
图67	万全威远东空台1　122
图68	万全威远东空台2　123
图69	万全西孤山　124
图70	万全洗马林倒V字墙　125
图71	万全洗马林长城席家窑段　126
图72	蔚县　127
图73	蔚县单堠堡关帝庙　128
图74	蔚县单堠村关帝庙东石表柱础顶部雕覆莲，腰部雕琴、棋　130
图75	蔚县单堠村关帝庙西石表柱础顶部雕覆莲，腰部雕书、画　131
图76	蔚县单堠村村外有堡壕，黄土夯筑的堡围墙　132
图77	蔚县单堠村堡门1　134
图78	蔚县单堠村堡门2　135
图79	蔚县单堠村内街巷　136
图80	蔚县古堡　138
图81	蔚县古堡影壁　139
图82	蔚县西大坪军堡　140
图83	蔚县羊圈堡军堡　142
图84	宣化　143
图85	宣化东望山乡葛峪堡点将台　144
图86	宣化凤凰山长城（石墙）　145
图87	宣化后坝村空心敌楼　146
图88	宣化青边口长城敌楼　147
图89	宣化青边口长城空心敌台挂绳梯处　148

图90　宣化青边口挂绳梯处细部图　149
图91　宣化青边口长城　150
图92　阳原　151
图93　阳原开阳古堡1　152
图94　阳原开阳古堡2　154
图95　阳原开阳古堡门　155
图96　阳原开阳古堡门匾额　156
图97　阳原马圈堡　157
图98　张北　158
图99　张北野狐岭　159
图100　张北正边台长城　160
图101　涿鹿　161
图102　涿鹿白家口敌台内景　162
图103　涿鹿白家口西门上方匾额　164
图104　涿鹿白家口壹号敌台箭窗　165
图105　涿鹿白家口龙字贰号敌台礌石孔　166
图106　涿鹿白家口龙字伍号敌台匾额　168
图107　涿鹿白家口龙字伍号敌台回廊　169
图108　涿鹿白家口龙字伍号敌台中心室拱券与储物室　170
图109　涿鹿白家口龙字陆号敌台　172
图110　涿鹿白家口龙字陆号敌台滚石口　173
图111　涿鹿白家口龙字敌台内台阶　174
图112　涿鹿龙字叁号敌台上旗杆石和水嘴　176
图113　涿鹿马水口叁号敌台内部结构图　177
图114　涿鹿马水口捌号敌台　178
图115　涿鹿马字拾号台匾额　180
图116　涿鹿马水口敌台条石基座与砖相接的四角石立柱载横卧条石与箭窗相接　181
图117　涿鹿马水口长城残存的箭窗　182
图118　涿鹿水头长城　184

长城主题创作
The Great Wall Theme Creation

图119　《长城之上》被河北美术馆收藏　187
图120　《长城脚下》　188
图121　《璀璨生辉》被河北省政府收藏　189

后记
Postscript

开篇小知识
The knowledge at the beginning

长城的名字

"长城"这个词最早出现在《管子》中,记载最早的长城是春秋战国时期的齐国因防御需要而修筑。在出土文物竹简、青铜器骉羌钟铭文中都有"长城"的记录,是实物佐证材料。

除此之外,关于长城还有一些不同的称谓,如《史记》中用到"堑""塞";《汉书·地理志》中用到"方城";《后汉书》记载"塞垣";《北史·契丹传》记载"长堑";《魏书》记载"塞围";《通典》记载"障塞";金代称"界壕""墙堑";《明史》记载"边""边墙""边垣""九边";历史文献中也有将"长城"与"塞""事障"等词合称表示长城的。

长城沿线因区域不同而产生浓浓的地方乡土韵味。宁夏民间将黄土夯筑的长城墩台称为"长城蛋蛋";明以前的长城被民间称为"土龙""黑土龙""黑地龙"等;蒙语中"乌尔科"专指"城墙""长城",这足以使我们感受到长城与生活息息相关。

The name of the Great Wall

The word "Great Wall" appeared in "Guanzi" first, which recorded that the earliest Great Wall was built by Qi during the Spring and Autumn period and the Warring States period for defense needs. There are many physical supporting materials such as the unearthed cultural relics bamboo slips, bronze ware, and Qiang bell inscriptions to record the "Great Wall".

In addition, there are many different names for the Great Wall, such as: "Qian" and "Sai" in the "Shi Ji", the "square city" in the "Han Book Geography", the "Saiyuan" in the "Hou Han Book", the "Chang Qian" in the "Bei History·Khitan Biography", the "Saiwei" in the "Wei Book", the "Zhangsai" in the "Tongdian", the "Jiehao" and "Qiangqian" in the Jin Dynasty, the "Bian", "Bian Wall", "Bianyuan", and "Jiubian" in the "History of the Ming Dynasty", and the "Changcheng", "Sai" and "Shizhang" in historical documents mean the Great Wall.

Different regions along the Great Wall have a strong local cultural feature. For instance, Ningxia folk call "Great Wall Dandan" to mean the Great Wall piers made of rammed loess. The Great Wall is also called "Tu Dragon", "Black Tu Dragon" and "Black Earth Dragon" etc. in the society before the Ming Dynasty. "Urko" means "city wall" and "Great Wall" in Mongolian. It is enough to feel that the Great Wall is closely related to life.

新中国的长城文化

中华人民共和国成立后对于长城的认知和定位经历了五个阶段，这五个阶段是递进的，使中国人民乃至世界对长城有了逐步完整和清晰的认识。

第一阶段，中华人民共和国成立后，长城文化觉醒，建立自信心。中国政府从1952年开始对长城开展分期分批的保护性修复工程。1971年，中国向联合国大会赠送一块万里长城大型挂毯，万里长城作为中华民族的象征，向世界传递着友好合作的愿望。

第二阶段，长城作为中华民族的骄傲被世界瞩目。国家领导人邓小平、习仲勋于1984年发出"爱我中华、修我长城"号召。1987年中国长城学会成立，第一任名誉会长习仲勋，会长黄华，使长城文化的保护工作逐渐加速。1987年12月，中国的万里长城列入《世界遗产名录》世界文化、自然双重遗产。世界遗产委员会评价：约公元前220年，一统天下的秦始皇将修建于早些时候的断续的防御工事连接成一个完整的防御系统，用以抵抗来自北方的侵略，明代（1368—1644）又继续加以修筑，使长城成为世界上最长的军事设施。它在文化艺术上的价值，足以与其在历史和战略上的重要性相媲美。

第三阶段，长城保护工作全面启动快速发展时期。2006年至2012年，颁发第一项关于中国长城的法律文件《长城保护条例》，全国长城资源调查与认定工作取得决定性成果；绘制完成全国长城分布图，涉及行经15个省404个县的长城遗迹43721处，共计21196.18公里。

第四阶段，长城保护深入研究科学规划。截至2016年9月，长城沿线所有省份共聘请4650名长城保护员。主要是三类群体：一类是致力于研究长城文化的专家学者；另一类是长城文化的爱好者，如摄影爱好者和自由撰稿人；最后一类是长城沿线自然村落的居民，高校教师的参与使长城文化的研究领域进一步拓宽。

第五阶段，自强不息，展望未来。《长城、大运河、长征国家文化公园建设方案》对长城科学保护、世代传承、合理利用等方面工作提出具体指导，要求到2023年年底完成建设任务。长城是中华民族的重要象征，它集物质、精神和文化于一体，承载着民族精神之根脉，是我们的先人贡献于全人类最伟大的思想文化宝库。关注这一宝库里的内在价值，揭示丰富的内涵，让中华民族的优秀文化和智慧传承于世，是一项永不停息的使命。

因张家口地处草原游牧民族和中原农耕民族地理上的天然分界线，是中国长城最早的修筑地之一。

The Great Wall Culture of New China

After the establishment of the People's Republic of China, the recognition and positioning of the Great Wall went through five stages. These stages are progressive. It also helps to have a fully clear complete understanding of the Great Wall for the Chinese people or even the whole world people.

In the first stage, after the establishment of the New China, the Great Wall Culture awakened to build up the country's self-confidence. Since 1952, the Chinese government began to carry out protective restoration projects on the Great Wall in phases. In 1971, China gave the United Nations General Assembly a large tapestry of the Great Wall, as a symbol of the Chinese nation, conveying the desire for friendly cooperation to the world.

In the second stage, the Great Wall attracted world attention as the pride of the Chinese nation. National leaders Deng Xiaoping and Xi Zhongxun issued a call to "love China and build the Great Wall" in 1984. The Great Wall Association of China was established in 1987 with the first honorary president Xi Zhongxun, and President Huang Hua, to gradually accelerate the protection of the Great Wall culture. In December 1987, the Great Wall of China was included in the World Heritage List as both world culture and world nature heritage. World Heritage Committee commented that Around 220 BC, Qin Shihuang, who ruled the world, connected a complete defense system with early intermittent fortifications. to resist invasion from the north. In the Ming Dynasty (1368-1644), the construction also continued and made the Great Wall the longest military installation in the world. Its cultural and artistic value can be comparable to its historical and strategic importance.

In the third stage, the protection work of the Great Wall has fully launched a period of rapid development. From 2006 to 2012, the first legal document on the Great Wall of China, the "Great Wall Protection Regulations" was issued. The national Great Wall resource survey and identification work have achieved decisive results. Also, the distribution map of the Great Wall across China has been drawn completely, involving 43,721 Great Wall ruins that pass through 404 counties in 15 provinces with a total of 21196.18 kilometers.

The fourth stage focused on the Great Wall protection in-depth study of scientific planning. All provinces along the Great Wall hired 4,650 Great Wall protectors before 2016 September. There were mainly three types of groups, firstly, it was about experts and scholars who were committed to studying the Great Wall. A group included amateurs of Great Wall culture, such as photography amateurs and freelance writers, and the third group included residents of natural villages along the Great Wall. The participation of university teachers has further broadened the research field of Great Wall Culture.

In the fifth stage, it keeps improving and looks forward to the future. The "Great Wall, Grand Canal, and the Long March National Cultural Park Construction Plan" focuses on the scientific protection, inheritance from generation to generation, and rational utilization of the Great Wall to provide specific guidance and require to complete the construction tasks by the end of 2023. The Great Wall is an important symbol of the Chinese nation. The Great Wall is an important symbol of the Chinese nation integrating material, spiritual, and cultural aspects, to carry the roots of the national spirit. It is also the greatest ideological and cultural treasure house contributed by our ancestors to all mankind. It is a never-ending mission to pay attention to the intrinsic value of this treasure house, revealing its rich connotations, and passing on the excellent culture and wisdom of the Chinese nation to the world.

Zhangjiakou is one of the earliest construction sites of the Great Wall of China with the reason of its location on the natural dividing line between the grassland nomads and the Central Plains farming people.

张家口被誉为历代长城"博物馆"

据河北省长城资源调查勘测统计,张家口长城及长城附属物遍布张家口各地,相关的历史事件被一代又一代的人口口相传至今。

张家口境内现存长城总长度达1804.846千米,为全国地市级中长城总长度最长;张家口境内始于战国时期的赵长城、燕长城经秦、汉、北魏、北齐、唐、金到明代、清代前后历经2000余年,时间跨度最大;张家口长城建造形制包含中国长城的所有建筑规制和建筑样式,相当于一本现实版的教科书;张家口境内有建造于东周末年的赵长城、燕长城,是目前全国规模最大、建筑年代最早并且保存最好的古长城;张家口赤城、崇礼、张北、沽源四地交界区域的长城,纵横交织,呈网状分布,是密度最大的长城群;张家口坝头一带的部分长城在前代的长城之上修缮,叠压多达五个朝代,为现存长城叠压最多;张家口桦皮岭和冰山梁区间的古长城建造在海拔2211米的山地,是最高的长城;张家口境内长城古驿道总里程最长;张家口市区加上13个县都有长城及长城附属建筑遗存;张家口现存长城遗迹包括烽火台2273座、敌台456座、关堡136座、古驿站22个、马面111座、相关遗存21处,数量为全国最多。

张家口曾经是历史上"最发达"的城市之一,是中国北方著名的陆路商道集散地;是中国最早对外开放的城市之一。边贸极为活跃,早在汉代设置榷场开始对外往来贸易,经过唐、宋、辽、金、元等时期到明朝形成较大规模。张家口大境门是长城四大重要关隘之一,建于清朝顺治元年,打破了长城沿线"城堡不开北门,修建关口不留门"的常规,兼具城关和城门的双重功能,汇集关内、关外的贸易和交通。正是因为这个特例,成就了张库大道的对外贸易鼎盛期。

Zhangjiakou is known as the "Museum" of the Great Wall of all dynasties.

According to statistics from the Great Wall Resources Survey in Hebei Province, the Zhangjiakou Great Wall and its attachments are spread throughout Zhangjiakou, and relevant historical events are taught by generations of people present.

The total length of the existing Great Wall in Zhangjiakou reaches 1,804.846 kilometers, which is the longest among the prefecture-level Great Walls in the country. Zhangjiakou Great Wall was the longest period starting from the Zhao Great Wall of the Zhanguo Dynasty and the Yan Great Wall to the Qin, Han, North Wei, North Qi, Tang, Jin, Min, and Qing Dynasties, more than 2,000 years. The construction form of the Great Wall of Zhangjiakou is a real-life textbook including all the architectural regulations and architectural styles of the Great Wall of China. Zhangjiakou has the Zhao Great Wall and the Yan Great Wall built in the Eastern Zhou Dynasty, which are currently the largest, oldest, and best-preserved ancient Great Walls in the country.

The Great Wall at the junction of Chicheng, Chongli, Zhangbei, and Guyuan in Zhangjiakou is the largest dense group of Great Walls with vertical and horizontal interweaving net-like distribution.

Part of the Great Wall in the Badou area of Zhangjiakou was renovated on top of the previous Great Wall, overlapping during as many as five dynasties. It is the most overlapping of the existing Great Wall. The ancient Great Wall between Huapi Ridge and Bingshanliang in Zhangjiakou is the highest Great Wall built on a mountain with an altitude of 2,211 meters. The total mileage of the Great Wall's ancient post roads in Zhangjiakou is the longest Great Wall.

The urban area of Zhangjiakou adds thirteen counties, having the remains of the Great Wall and its ancillary buildings. The existing Great Wall remains in Zhangjiakou and is the largest number in the country including 2,273 beacon towers, 456 enemy towers, 136 Guanbao, 22 ancient post stations, 111 horse faces, and 21 related relics.

Zhangjiakou was one of the "most developed" cities in history once, and a distribution center for the famous overland trade routes in northern China. It is the first city in China to open to the outside world. For instance, the border trade is extremely active. As early as the Han Dynasty, the establishment of the market began to exchange trade with foreign countries. After the Tang, Song, Liao, Jin, and Yuan Dynasties, it formed a large scale in the Ming Dynasty. Zhangjiakou Dajing Gate is one of the four important gates of the Great Wall. It was built in the first year of Shunzhi in the Qing Dynasty. The castle along the Great Wall does not open the north gate, and the gates are built without leaving the gate. It has the dual functions of all gates and gathers trade and traffic inside and outside the gate. It is precisely because of this special case that the foreign trade of Zhangku Avenue was achieved in the flourishing period of trading.

长城的修建原则

修建长城时在选址、布局和施工等方面都要遵循一定的原则。

通过观察山东、河南、河北、陕西、内蒙古等地的春秋战国长城遗迹，发现春秋战国时期初步建立长城沿线军事防御配置的选址和布局都遵循了一些基本原则。秦汉时期，各种布防基本实施方法进一步明确，但没有严格的定式。直到明朝才形成较为严格的规定，在各个方面完善并且规范。

The Great Wall's Construction Principles

The construction of the Great Wall follows certain principles in terms of site selection, layout, and construction.

By observing the remains of the Great Wall in the Spring and Autumn Period and the Warring States Period in Shandong, Henan, Hebei, Shaanxi, Inner Mongolia, and other places. Some basic principles were initially established for the site selection and layout of the military defense configuration along the Great Wall. During the Qin and Han dynasties, the basic implementation methods of various defense deployments were further clarified, but there was no strict formula. The Ming Dynasty formed relatively strict regulations. And they were perfected and standardized in all aspects.

以险制塞的空间原则

"因地形，用制险塞"是历代修筑长城普遍采用的重要指导原则。是根据所经之处战略重要性和地形的不同特点，按实际情况灵活确定长城的走向、建筑的体量、选用的材料等因地制宜的方式进行规划设计施工。

长城作为军事防御工程，是人工构筑的军事防御系统和山脊、沟谷、河流、平原等自然险阻有机结合。选择冲要位置易守难攻的地方设置关隘，采用石块垒砌、劈山就险、自然山险、深沟高垒等多种形式修建高大、坚固且连绵不断的长城墙体来强化自然险阻，在山体非常险峻、敌人很难上去的地方，基本无须人工修筑墙体。古人巧妙地利用山险，甚至采取铲削山崖的办法来加强山险。在平原、草地、沙丘地带则采用黄土夯筑、砂石混筑、垒墙、筑城，使长城在平坦的旷野中延伸，达到有效防御的目的。充分利用地形，将墙体与山崖、峭壁、沟壑、峡谷、河流、森林等自然险阻相连，形成一道人造工程与天然地形互相补充的军事防御线。以险制塞的空间原则，保证了长城防御作用的有效发挥。

The spatial principle of danger control fortresses

"Using the terrain as the danger block" was an important guiding principle commonly used in the construction of the Great Wall in the past dynasties.

It was based on the strategic importance of the place and the different characteristics of the terrain, the direction of the Great Wall, the volume of the building, the selected materials, etc. Also, they were flexibly determined according to the actual situation. Planning, design, and construction are carried out according to local conditions.

As a military defense project, the Great Wall was an organic combination of an artificial military defense system and natural obstacles such as ridges, valleys, rivers, and plains.

It was easy to choose a strategic location and defend but difficult to attack. Then, it helped to set up a security camp and build tall, strong, and continuous Great Wall walls in various forms such as stone building, mountain-splitting, natural mountain barriers, deep ditches, and high bases to strengthen natural obstacles. The mountains were very steep and it is difficult for the enemy to go up. There was no need to build walls manually. The ancients cleverly used the mountain danger, and even took the method of shoveling cliffs to strengthen mountain dangers.

In the plains, grasslands, and dunes, rammed loess, sand and gravel construction, fortified walls, and fortifications were used to extend the Great Wall in the flat wilderness to achieve the purpose of effective defense.

Making full of the terrain and connecting the wall with natural obstacles such as cliffs, ravines, canyons, rivers, forests, etc. to form a military defense line with man-made engineering projects and natural terrain complements. The spatial principle of preventing danger blockage ensured the effective performance of the defensive role of the Great Wall.

就地取材的施工原则

建筑材料是修建长城的物质基础。在天然险阻要地修建长城既要考虑坚固实用，又要考虑节约人力、物力，因此历代长城修建都遵循就地取材的原则。在具体施工中，根据各个地域特有的自然环境状况及不同的气候条件选用建筑材料，避免长距离运输，充分依靠本地资源，发挥材料契合的特性，降低人力、物力等施工成本，充分做到"就地取材，因材施用"。

据石刻碑文记载，明朝修建长城按三个等级建造。不同等级的长城有着相同的特点，共同点是就地取材和因地制宜；不同的是材料选择和加工技术。

一等长城多修在要塞部位，一般以方条石为基座，墙身内外两侧用砖或条石砌筑，墙心填以灰土夯筑或毛石砌体，上部的垛口和女墙一律用砖砌出，墙顶也用砖铺墁，以供人马行走。

二等长城墙身外侧用砖或条石砌筑，内部用毛石砌体，内侧表面做虎皮石墙面，并用白灰勾缝。垛口及女墙全部用砖砌筑，墙顶也用砖铺墁。

三等长城一般用毛石砌筑，内外两侧表面均做虎皮石墙面，墙的厚度、断面尺寸及墙顶上部的做法均根据防御需要和地形条件而定。

Construction principles of local materials

Building materials were the material basis for the construction of the Great Wall. To build the Great Wall in a natural and dangerous place, we must consider not only its sturdiness and practicality but also the saving of manpower and material resources. Therefore, the construction of the Great Wall in the past dynasties must follow the principle of using local materials. In the specific construction, building materials were selected according to the unique natural environment and different climatic conditions of each region to avoid long-distance transportation, fully relying on local resources, to give characteristics of materials. It also helped to reduce construction costs such as manpower and material resources, and fully achieve "The materials were collected locally and applied according to the materials."

According to stone inscriptions, the Ming Dynasty built the Great Wall on three levels. The Great Wall of different grades had the use of local materials and adaption measures to local conditions. And the difference is in material selection and processing technology.

The first-class Great Walls were mostly built in the fortress, usually with square stone as the base. The inner and outer sides of the wall were built with bricks or strips of stone. The center of the wall is filled with rammed soil or rubble masonry. The upper crenel and upper parapet were all made of bricks, and the tops of the walls were also paved with bricks for people and horses to walk.

The outer side of the second-class Great Wall was built with bricks or strips of stone. The interior was made of rubble masonry, and the inner surface was made of tiger skin stone wall with white ash jointing. The crenels and parapet walls are all built with bricks, and the tops of the walls were also paved with bricks.

The third-class Great Wall was generally built with rubble. Both the inner and outer surfaces were made of tiger-skin stone walls. The thickness of the wall, the size of the section, and the upper part of the wall were determined, according to the defense needs and terrain conditions.

纵深防御的布局原则

北方游牧骑兵对长城防线构成威胁,长城防守需要找到解除这种军事压力的方法,以保证一道前线被攻破之后,还有多重防线进行抵御。因此,纵深防御成为长城修建的一项布局原则。纵深防御的作用是在敌方突破长城防线后,阻止其长驱直入,迅速深入到长城防御方的腹地。每一道长城防线都是相对独立的体系,可以独立作战。只要几条防线中有一道防线不失守,就能有效阻挡进攻的敌人。此外,后边的防线可以向前支援,加强阻挡敌人的力量。已经被攻破的防线,可以尽快地形成新的防御力量,对进攻的敌人采取包抄、倒打、围堵、截断退路等战术。在张家口、大同、偏关一带有头边、二边、三边、四边,是加强防御的不同防线。

The layout principles of defense in depth

The northern nomadic cavalry posed a threat to the defense line of the Great Wall. The defense of the Great Wall needed to find a way to relieve this military pressure to ensure that after a front line is broken. There were multiple lines of defense to resist. Therefore, defense in depth had become a layout principle for the construction of the Great Wall.

The function of the defense in depth prevented the enemy from driving straight after breaking through the defense line of the Great Wall and quickly penetrating the hinterland of the Great Wall defender. Each Great Wall defense line was a relatively independent system and could operate independently. As long as one of the several defense lines is not lost, it could effectively block the attacking enemy. In addition, the defense back line could support forward to strengthen the enemy resistance. The defense lines that had been broken to form a new defense force as soon as possible. and took tactics such as outflanking, overthrowing, encircling, and cutting off retreat routes against the attacking enemy. In Zhangjiakou, Datong, and Pianguan, the first side, second side, third side, and fourth side were different lines of defense to strengthen defense.

长城纵深防御建构的原则

通常要在长城城堡的外侧设置一些障碍物，如城墙、壕堑等，在长城内外沿线设有镇城、卫城、所城、关城、城堡、烽火台等。这些不同形制、用途各异的防御设施，与线性长城墙体互相配合，连成一个有机的、纵深的、严密的和连续的长城防御整体。

战略重镇的长城修建讲求多道重层，扩大防御纵深，形成立体作战的空间收缩原则。在战略要地，长城防御体系设置更加周密，在经过的交通要地设立关隘，派重兵严密防守，并且在各种防御设施基础上在长城内外大量增加修建城堡，用于驻扎守军，从而满足纵深防御的需要。

在草场、河道等相对开阔的区域，地势并不险峻，易攻难守，采取加大防御纵深的办法来弥补这种劣势。

Principles of the Great Wall's Defense-in-Depth Construction

Some obstacles should be usually set up on the outside of the Great Wall Castle, such as city walls, trenches, etc. There were towns, acropolises, fortresses, gates, castles, beacon towers, etc. along the inside and outside of the Great Wall, inner and outer lines. These defense facilities of different shapes and purposes cooperated with the linear Great Wall structure to form an organic, deep, tight, and continuous Great Wall defense as a whole.

The construction of the Great Wall in a strategic town emphasized multiple layers to expand the depth of defense and forms the principle of space contraction for three-dimensional operations. The defense system of the Great Wall at strategic locations was more elaborate. Passes had been set up at important transportation points, and heavy troops were deployed for tight defense. Based on various defense facilities, a large number of castles had been built inside and outside of the Great Wall for station defenders, to meet the needs of depth of defense needs.

In relative opening areas such as grasslands and rivers, the terrain was not steep easy to attack, and difficult to defend. The method of increasing the depth of defense was adopted to make up for this disadvantage.

分段承包的施工原则

　　长城的修建多是由相关机构拨付经费并组织施工，其原则多是采取分段承包施工方式。在修建长城的过程中，参与施工的人多，时间周期较长，所以施工管理是一项很复杂的工作。为便于管理，历代修建长城多采取分段包干、各负其责的办法。明代修筑长城时实行严格的责任制，即采用分区、分片、分段包干的办法，材料的征集也是分派到防区内的各部队甚至是州县。

　　历代修建长城的主要力量大多是军队，按照军事管理的不同级别逐级分解施工任务，两个相邻的施工单位有明确的衔接地点。将一个较大的队伍划分成为多个施工小组，每个施工团队完成其所担负的长城修建任务后，指挥机构再将他们派到下一个地段去修筑城墙。

Construction principles of segmented contracting

The construction of the Great Wall was mostly funded and organized by relevant institutions. The construction of the Great Wall was mostly based on the principle of segmented contract construction.

In the process of building the Great Wall, there were many people involved in the construction and the period was long. Construction management was a very complicated task. To facilitate management, the construction of the Great Wall in the past dynasties mostly adopted the method of sub-contracting and taking responsibility for each. When building the Great Wall in the Ming Dynasty, a strict responsibility system was implemented, that was the method of zoning, fragmentation, and section contracting was adopted.

The main force in the construction of the Great Wall in the past dynasties was mostly the military. Construction tasks were broken down step by step according to the different levels of military management. Two adjacent construction units had clear connection points. A larger team was divided into multiple construction teams. After each construction team completes its task of building the Great Wall, the command agency would send them to the next section to build the wall.

"物勒工名"

"物勒工名"即对长城工程实行责任制管理。为确保长城修建工程的质量，明代隆庆时期以后开始在长城修建记事碑，上刻文字说明，包括承包单位修筑长城的位置、形制等相关信息，还刻有负责长城修建的各级官员的官衔、姓名、所属单位、施工组织者及施工人员的姓名，有些甚至细化到将石匠、泥瓦匠、木匠、铁匠、窑匠等的姓名都刻在碑上。

"Wule Gongming"

Wule Gongming meant implementing responsibility management for the Great Wall Project.
To ensure the quality of the Great Wall construction project, after the Longqing period of the Ming Dynasty, text descriptions were engraved on the monuments of the Great Wall construction, including the location and shape of the contracting units to build the Great Wall and other relevant information, as well as the official titles and names of officials at all levels responsible for the construction of the Great Wall, the name of the unit and the construction personnel. Some were even refined to engrave the names of the stonemasons, masons, carpenters, blacksmiths, potters, etc. on the tablets.

长城的构成形式

长城并不是简单孤立的一道城墙。长城是根据纵深防御的原则进行布局，由长城本体、附属建筑及相关建筑、设施等共同组成，包括墙体、墙台、敌台、烽火台、水口门、关口障城等建筑。由点到线、由线到面，将长城沿线的关隘、墙体、关城和城堡等相关建筑相连接，起到较为理想的防御作用，以利于农耕民族在一个相对有安全保障的空间里从事农业生产。

The composition of the Great Wall

The Great Wall was not a simple isolated city wall. It was laid out according to the principle of defense in depth and consisted of the Great Wall itself, ancillary buildings, and related buildings and facilities including walls, wall platforms, enemy towers, beacon towers, water gates, passes, barriers, and other buildings. From point to line, and from line to surface, connecting the passes, walls, gates, castles, and other related buildings along the Great Wall played an ideal defensive role. To facilitate the farming people to engage in a relatively safe space and agricultural production.

长城本体

长城本体既是长城的主体，又是长城军事防御体系的核心部分，主要有墙体、列燧。

根据长城所处的地理环境、位置等条件，选择不同的建筑材料，采用不同的建造方式，目的是既节约人力、物力，又提高修建的速度。例如，如果有充足的黄土可以烧制青砖，则附近长城多为青砖包砌；如果采石比较方便，则附近的长城主要是石砌城墙。长城墙体建筑主要采取三种方式，即石砌、土夯、砖包。长城的墙体因建造材料和地势的不同而形制各异，分为土墙、石墙、砖墙、木障墙、山险墙及山险、河险等多种形式。

土墙是使用以土为主要材料修建的墙体。根据建造方式的不同，土墙又分为堆土墙、夯工墙、土坯墙、红柳或芦苇夹沙墙几种类型。

木障墙是用木栅栏建成的防御性工事。明辽东边墙东段即为木障墙。

Great Wall body

It was not only the main body of the Great Wall but also the core part of the Great Wall's military defense system. The main body of the Great Wall mainly consisted of walls and columns.

According to the geographical environment, location, and other conditions of the Great Wall, different building materials were selected and different construction methods were adopted. The purpose was to save manpower and material resources and improved the speed of construction. For example, if there was enough loess to burn green bricks, the nearby Great Wall would mostly be made of green bricks. If quarrying was more convenient, the nearby Great Wall would mainly be made of stone walls. There were three main ways to build the walls of the Great Wall, namely stone masonry, earth ramming, and brick cladding. The walls of the Great Wall had different shapes due to different construction materials and terrain.

Earth walls were walls built with soil as the main material. According to the different construction methods, earth walls were divided into several types such as earth pile walls, rammed walls, adobe walls, tamarisks, or reed sand walls.

A wooden barrier wall was a defensive fortification built with wooden fences. The eastern section of the Ming-Liao east border wall was the wooden barrier wall.

附建在长城本体上的结构设施

除长城本体之外,还有一些附建于其上的设施,主要包括垛口、女墙、障墙、瞭望孔、射孔、礌石孔、排水口和敌台(敌楼)、铺舍、马面、马道及登城步道等。

Structural facilities attached to the Great Wall itself.

In addition to the Great Wall itself, there were also some facilities attached to it, mainly including crenels, parapets, barrier walls, lookout holes, perforations, stone holes, drainage outlets, and enemy towers. (watch towers), pavilions, horse faces, horse paths, climbing trails, etc.

障墙

　　障墙是修建在长城墙体顶部、与墙体垂直的横向短墙，只留下较窄的通道，障墙上常设瞭望孔和射孔，便于遮蔽守城士兵。主要用于观察敌情，当某段城墙被敌人攻克时能够从双向夹击，射杀敌兵，收复失地。中国人民革命军事博物馆古代兵器馆中的塞门刀车是机械兵器，可以形成一段横档，把敌人限制在一定区域内消灭，相当于可移动的障墙。

The barrier wall

The barrier wall was built on the top of the Great Wall, with a short horizontal wall perpendicular to the wall, leaving only a narrow passage. Lookout holes and perforations were often installed on the barrier wall to facilitate shielding the defenders. It was mainly used to observe the enemy's situation. When a certain section of the city wall was captured by the enemy, it could attack from both directions and shoot the enemy soldiers to regain the lost ground. The Semen Knife Cart in the Ancient Weapons Hall of the Military Museum of the Chinese People's Revolution was a mechanical weapon that could form a rung to confine the enemy to a certain area and eliminate it. It was equivalent to a movable barrier wall.

其他相关建筑

作为军事防御工事，长城除本体及附建于本体上的建筑和设施外，还包括本体之外的一系列相关建筑及设施，如关隘、城堡、戍堡、住所、驿站、烽火台、火池、烟灶、挡马墙、天田、砖瓦窑、水窖、驿道等。这些建筑及设施对长城本体起到保障、支援等作用，在很大程度上强化了长城本体的防御功能，使长城这道防线更具抵御入侵的作用。

瓮城，亦称月城。是附建于关门外侧的小城，平面呈半圆形或方形，瓮城两侧的墙体与关城城墙相连，构成一个内部封闭的空间。瓮城一般建有箭楼、门闸、垛门等设施。

天田是长城的配套和辅助性设施，一般在长城内侧将土地犁松或铺上细沙，用以观察脚印、判断敌情并及时发现敌方踪迹。

砖瓦窑是烧制砖瓦等建筑材料的设施。长城沿线的砖瓦窑主要是为长城本体、城堡，以及其他建筑及设施提供所需的砖瓦等建筑材料。按照需要，采用黏土作为原料，所以砖瓦窑主要建在长城途经的黄土、黄褐土地带。

长城的历史是不同朝代、不断修筑和使用长城的过程，这与中国古代王朝的经济结构和政治结构有关，修建和使用长城的政治及经济基础体现当时的社会发展特点及规律。不同朝代长城的修建要满足其社会经济、政治稳定的需要。长城不断修建于农牧经济利益的冲突地带，即农耕与游牧交错地带，所以调整农牧经济利益冲突是长城防御的任务之一。长城在化解游牧和农耕冲突与矛盾中所发挥的作用，主要体现在为双方良性互动提供基础条件。有了长城的存在，也就有了稳定和寻求和平解决利益冲突的基础。

早在汉代，长城边关就已经开设关市，当时的贸易项目有牛马和布匹等。唐、宋、元等朝代的马市贸易都很发达，明代所设的马市最多。马市虽然有时开有时停，规模大小不一，但作为农牧经济双向贸易交流渠道，总体上处于运转常态。明朝"隆庆和议"之后在长城地区出现长时间的和平局面，双方冲突的概率降低，双方在利益表达、利益平衡方面更容易通过协商谈判的方式来实现，更容易找到双方都可获益的途径。在双方利益都得到保证的框架下，寻求一种制度化的妥协，从而达到双赢的目的，形成长城内外不同的利益主体互利共存的关市，收买马匹、粮食、茶叶等物品。据史籍记载，张家口一带"南京罗绫铺、苏杭绸缎铺、潞州绸铺、泽州帕铺，临清布帛铺、绒丝铺、杂货铺，各行交易，铺沿长四五里许"。马市在满足双方生产和生活需要的同时，也在客观上起到缓解农牧冲突的作用。

随着长城内外农耕与游牧贸易的发展，关市开放的范围越来越广，规模和次

Other related buildings

As a military fortification, the Great Wall includes not only the main body, the buildings and facilities attached to the main body, but also a series of related buildings and facilities other than the main body, such as passes, castles, forts, residences, post stations, beacon tower, fire pools, smoke stove, horse retaining wall, Tiantian, brick kiln, water cellar, post road, etc. These buildings and facilities play a role in protecting and supporting the Great Wall itself to a large extent strengthening the defensive function of the Great Wall itself. This makes the Great Wall's line of defense more effective in resisting invasion.

The Weng City, also known as the Moon City, is a small city attached to the outside of the gate. It is semicircular or square in plan. The walls on both sides of Weng City are connected to the Guan City wall to construct an internal closed space. Weng City generally has facilities such as arrow towers, and gates.

The supporting and auxiliary facilities of the Tiantian Great Wall generally plowed the land or spread fine sand on the inside of the Great Wall to observe footprints, judge the enemy's situation, and discover enemy traces in time.

The brick kiln is a facility for firing bricks and other building materials. The brick and tile kilns along the Great Wall mainly provide bricks, tiles, and other building materials needed for the Great Wall itself, castles, other buildings and facilities. Clay is used as the raw material according to needs, so, brick and tile kilns are mainly built in the loess and yellow-brown soil areas along the Great Wall.

The history of the Great Wall is a process of continuous construction and use of the Great Wall in different dynasties. This is related to the economic and political structure of ancient Chinese dynasties. The political and economic basis for the construction and use of the Great Wall reflects the characteristics and laws of social development at that time. The construction of the Great Wall in different dynasties must meet their socio-economic and political stability needs. The Great Wall is continuously built in the conflict zone of agricultural and pastoral economic interests, that is, the intersection between farming and nomadic life. Therefore, adjusting the conflict of agricultural economic interests is one of the tasks of the Great Wall defense. The role played by the Great Wall in resolving conflicts and contradictions between nomadism and farming is mainly reflected in providing basic conditions for good interaction between the two parties. With the existence of the Great Wall, there is a basis for stability and the pursuit of peaceful resolution of conflicts of interest.

As early as the Han Dynasty, customs markets had been set up at the Great Wall border gates, and trade items at that time included cattle, horses, and cloth. The horse market trade was very developed in the Tang, Song, Yuan, and other dynasties. The Ming Dynasty had the largest number of horse markets. Although the horse market sometimes opened and sometimes stopped, and varied in size, as a two-way trade exchange channel for the agricultural and animal husbandry economy, it was generally operating normally. The long-term peaceful situation that emerged in the Great Wall area after the "Longqing Peace Conference" in the Ming Dynasty reduced the probability of conflict between the two parties. It was easier for both parties to express and balance their interests through consultation and negotiation, and it was easier to find a solution that could benefit both parties. Under the framework where the interests of both parties are guaranteed, an institutionalized compromise was sought to achieve a win-win goal, to achieve the mutually beneficial coexistence of different stakeholders inside and outside the Great Wall, and to purchase horses, grain, tea, and other items. According to historical records, in the

数也更大更多。明代马市的发展以"隆庆和议"为分水岭，分为前后两个时期。前一时期以明蒙之间官办的"朝贡优赏贸易"为主，后一时期马市性质发生变化，发展成为互市贸易，从官市过渡到民市，在更大规模的贸易市场上，民间自相往来、互通有无占据了主导地位。

明隆庆五年（1571）以后，长城沿线除辽东原有马市外，九边各镇又开设11处马市。其中，大同有3处，即得胜口、新平、守口；在宣府有1处，即张家口宣化；在山西有1处，即水泉营；在延绥有1处，即红山寺堡；在宁夏有3处，即清水营、中卫、平虏卫；在甘肃有2处，即洪水扁都口、高沟寨。这些都是每年只开一次的官市，在当时称为"大市"，属定期定额的贸易往来。按月开放的"民市"，贸易交流的物资更多样，属于官府监督之下民间的贸易行为，当时称为"小市"。

明朝对各地方马市的开放时间和规模都有明确的规定。早期规定每月开放一次，由初一到初五。再到每月开放两次，分别为初一到初五、十六到二十。到万历时马市开市的次数越来越多，在一些地方甚至出现不闭市的状况，而且交易品种越来越多，交易量也越来越大。从长城外到关市来进行贸易，要带着马匹等贸易货物到指定的地方进行官验，获得批准后才能进入市场。牧民到长城关隘进行马的交易，首先要由市场管理机构认定马的等级，马的价钱根据马的等级而确定。明永乐元年（1403）将马分为上上马、上马、中马、下马、驹五种。上上马一匹可以换绢八匹、布十二匹。到永乐十五年（1417）重新规定马的价钱，上上马可以换米五石、布绢各五匹。官市之外的民市，原则上由贸易双方自由议价。长城以内的人可以用农具、服饰、粮谷、铁锅等交换牧民的马、牛、羊、毛皮、人参等。隆庆五年五月至八月，明朝先后在大同得胜堡、宣府张家口堡、大同新平堡、山西水泉营堡开设马市，朝廷以银购马，另有很丰厚的抚赏。

清朝初期，茶马互市沿袭明制。但随着清朝在全国范围内统治秩序的建立，社会安定，民间贸易繁盛，茶法、马政也开始发生相应的变化，以往由官方指定的互市形式逐渐被空前广泛的民间自由贸易所取代。

长城，被列为中古世界七大奇观之一。是中华民族坚强不屈精神力量的象征，是人类历史文化瑰宝。

长城学是从总体上对长城进行综合研究的一门学科，属于认识论。是在许多相关学科的研究成果之上，对文献史料和考古材料的整理及遗址、遗迹的考察研究。

研究内容包括：提高对长城研究宏观上的认识，不断拓展研究领域；运用多学科的知识和研究方法，提高对长城的宏观认知能力。研究的目的：利用研究长城遗存及建筑的年代历史的标尺，提供参考数据，解析并防治沙漠化和水土流失

Zhangjiakou area, there were "Nanjing Luo Ling Shop, Suhang Silk Shop, Luzhou Silk Shop, Zezhou Pa Shop; Linqing Silk Shop, Velvet Silk Shop, Grocery Shop, and various trade shops with a length of about four or five miles long." The horse market not only met the production and living needs of both parties but also objectively played a role in alleviating agricultural and animal husbandry conflicts.

With the development of farming and nomadic trade inside and outside the Great Wall, the scope of Guan City opening became wider and wider, and the scale and frequency became larger and more frequent. The development of the horse market in the Ming Dynasty took the "Longqing Peace Conference" as the watershed and was divided into two major periods. The former period was dominated by the government-run "tribute and reward trade" between the Ming and Mongolia. In the latter period, the nature of the horse market changed and developed into mutual market trade had transitioned from the official market to the private market. In the larger-scale trade market, private exchanges and exchanges of supplies had taken a dominant position.

After the fifth year of Longqing's reign in the Ming Dynasty (1571), in addition to the original horse market in Liaodong, eleven more horse markets were opened in the towns of Jiubian along the Great Wall. There were three places, Deshengkou, Xinping, and Shoukou in Datong. There was one place, Xuanhua in Zhangjiakou in Xuanfu. There was one place in Shanxi, called Shuiquanying. There was one place in Yansui, called Hongshan Temple Fort, and three places in Ningxia, called Qingshuiying, Zhongwei, and Pingluwei. There were two places in Gansu, called Biandukou and Gaogouzhai. These were official markets that only opened once a year. They were called "big markets" at that time, and they were regular trade transactions with restricted periods and limited budgets. The "civilian market" opened monthly, and the materials for trade and exchange were more diverse. It was a private trade activity under the supervision of the government and was called a "small market" at that time.

The Ming Dynasty had clear regulations on the opening hours and scale of local horse markets. In the early days, it was stipulated that it would be open once a month from the first to the fifth day of the lunar month. Then, it would be open twice a month from the first to the fifth day of the lunar month, and from the 16th to the 20th day of the lunar month. In the Wanli period, the number of civil market openings was increasing, and in some places, the market was even open. There were more and more types of transactions, and the transaction volume was also increasing. Moreover, when people came from outside the Great Wall to trade in Guan City, they must bring horses and other trade goods to a designated place for official inspection. They could only enter the market after obtaining approval. When Herdsmen went to the Great Wall Pass to trade horses, they must be certified by the market management agency first. The price of the horse was determined based on the grade of the horse. In the first year of Yongle in the Ming Dynasty (1403), horses were divided into five classes top-level horse, upper-level horse, middle-level horse, lower-level horse, and colt. Top-level horses could exchange for eight pieces of silk and twelve pieces of cloth. In the 15th year of Yongle (1417), the price of horses was re-stipulated. The price of top-level horses could be exchanged for five packages of rice and five pieces of cloth and silk. Theoretically, in the private market other than the official market, both parties could freely negotiate prices. Within the Great Wall, people could exchange agricultural tools, clothing, grains, iron pots, etc. for herdsmen's horses, cattle, sheep, furs, ginseng, etc. From May to August in the fifth year of Longqing, the Ming Dynasty opened horse markets in Desheng Fort in Datong, Zhangjiakou Fort in Xuanfu, Xinping Fort in Datong, and Shuiquanying Fort in Shanxi. The court purchased horses with silver and received generous rewards.

问题；旅游经济学，为长城文化游提供理论依据。

长城学研究的范围：

1. 长城的走径、控制范围与地理环境的关系密切。

2. 建造年代是始建还是改建或重建。

3. 对长城的基本调查，掌握时间节点及空间坐标方面的真实数据、时代风貌。补充历史的记载。

4. 长城史料的整理和编纂。地方志书、通史、典章、碑刻、专著等文献中，散见于诗文、笔记；

5. 军事史和军事科学方面的研究；

6. 经济史方面的研究；

7. 历史地理学方面的研究；

8. 民族学方面的研究；

9. 建筑学方面的研究；

10. 旅游开发方面的研究；

11. 关于长城保护维修方面的研究。

长城学研究方法：

1. 文献考据法。首先是阅读、收集、科学整理和系统分析，地方志尤为重要，互证。

2. 野外考察法。主要是采取考古的方法，首先是广泛深入地普查，如照相、测绘草图、文字记录等地层记录，还要针对建筑物、烽燧、城堡中的物质文化、生活遗存充分挖掘收集。

3. 航空遥感技术的应用。此技术具有资源勘查和自然灾害监测方面的优势。因长城分布地区广，交通不便，地势险要，现场损毁程度具有较大的不可知性。

4. 社会学的研究方法。还原时代背景，从社会学的角度分析问题，多维度地分析问题，拓展长城研究的领域，如与长城相关联的建筑实体与历史事件、人物、思想、制度等有机整体。

In the early Qing Dynasty, the tea-horse trade followed the Ming system. However, with the establishment of the Qing Dynasty's nationwide ruling order, social stability, the prosperity of private trade, tea laws, and horse administration also began to experience corresponding changes. The mutual trading forms designated by the government in the past were gradually replaced by unprecedentedly extensive private free trade.

The Great Wall is listed as one of the seven wonders of the medieval world. It is a symbol of the indomitable spiritual power of the Chinese nation and a treasure of human history and culture.

Great Wall Studies is a discipline of epistemology that conducts comprehensive research on the Great Wall as a whole. It is based on the research results of many related disciplines including the compilation of historical documents and archaeological materials and the investigation and research of sites and remains.

The research content includes improving the macro-level understanding of the Great Wall research and continuously expanding the research field, using multi-disciplinary knowledge and research methods to improve the macro-cognitive ability of the Great Wall. The purpose of the research is to provide reference data to analyze and prevent desertification and soil erosion problems using the chronological and historical remains and buildings of the Great Wall. Tourism economics provides a theoretical basis for cultural tourism of the Great Wall.

The scope of research on Great Wall Studies includes:

1. The route and control range of the Great Wall, and it is closely related to the geographical environment. 2. Construction year: it was first built, renovated or rebuilt. 3. Basic survey of the Great Wall, mastering real data on time nodes and spatial coordinates, and the style of times, with supplement historical records. 4. The collation and compilation of historical materials on the Great Wall. Local chronicles, general histories, statutes, inscriptions, monographs, and other documents are scattered in poems and notes. 5. Researching on military history and military science. 6. Researching on economic history. 7. Researching on historical geography. 8. Researching on ethnic groups. 9. Researching on architecture. 10. Researching on tourism development of the Great Wall. 11. Researching on the protection and maintenance of the Great Wall.

Researching methods of Great Wall Studies.

1. Literature research method, first of all, it includes reading, collection, scientific organization, and systematic analysis, local chronicles are particularly important for mutual verification. 2. The field investigation method, mainly adopts archaeological methods. Firstly, it is an extensive and in-depth census, stratigraphic records such as photography, surveying sketches, written records, etc. It is also necessary to fully excavate and collect the material culture and life remains in buildings, beacons, and castles. 3. Application of aerial remote sensing technology. This technology has advantages in resource exploration and natural disaster monitoring. Because of the wide distribution area of the Great Wall, inconvenient transportation, dangerous terrain, and the extent of on-site damage are highly unpredictable. 4. Sociological research methods. Restoring the background of the times, analyzing problems from a sociological perspective, analyzing problems in multiple dimensions, and expanding the field of Great Wall research. The architectural entities associated with the Great Wall, have an organic integrity such as historical events, characters, ideas, systems, etc.

画卷徐徐展开
The scroll slowly unfolds

01

图1　赤城
Figure 1　Chicheng

02

图2 赤城长伸地堡长城

Figure 2 Chicheng Changshen Bunker Great Wall

鸟瞰式构图，一览全貌。取当地山石之土，夯筑守护家园的城墙。

A bird's-eye view of the composition, at a glance. Take the soil from the local mountains and rocks, to build a city wall to protect the homeland.

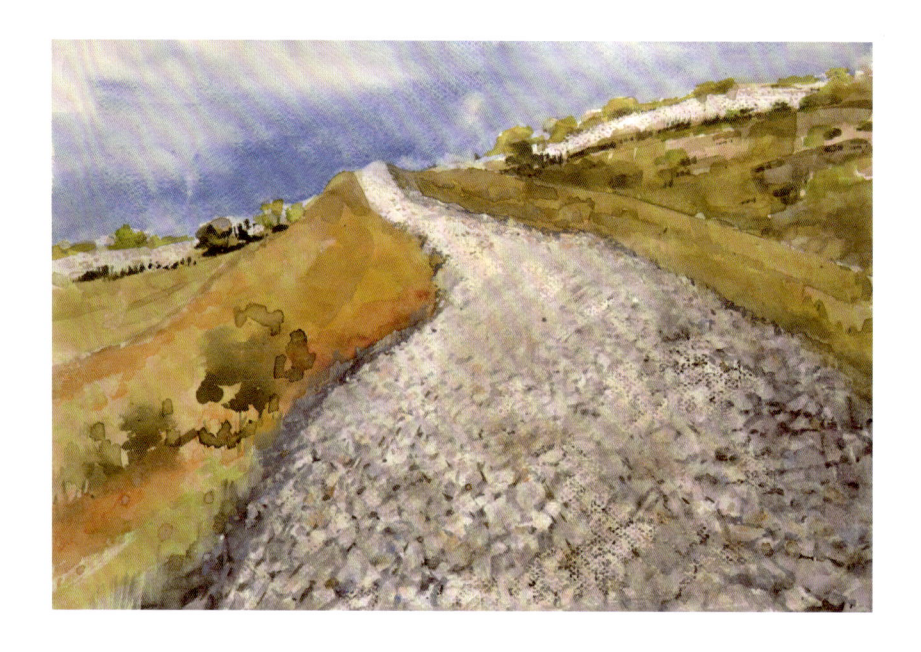

03

图3 赤城冰山梁长城
Figure 3   Chicheng Bingshanliang Great Wall

依山坡走势以碎石铺筑，又称毛石干垒墙。毛石是指自然形成、未经人工分拣的石头，石块之间不用泥土黏结。这类墙体主要建造在石质的山地上。

According to the trend of the hillside, it is paved with gravel, also known as rubble drywall. Rubble refers to stones that are naturally formed and have not been sorted by humans. The stones do not need to be bonded with soil. This type of wall is mainly built on rocky mountains.

04

图4 赤城雕鹗土筑长城

Figure 4　The Great Wall built with carved soil in Chicheng

  夯土墙是用木板做夹板，把经过筛选而能够黏合在一起的土壤填塞其中，然后将虚土夯实形成长城墙体。

  夯土筑造，夹层为小石头块，又称堆土夯筑，在堆土时逐层使用石质或木质的夯、杵等工具，反复、细密地夯砸，以使土质紧密、牢固。这类墙体主要建在地表为土质的地带，分布范围比较广，是长城建造的主要方式。

The rammed earth wall is made of wooden boards as plywood, filled with soil that has been screened and can be bonded together, and then compacts the empty soil to form the Great Wall.

Built with rammed earth, the interlayer is made of small stones, also known as rammed earth. Stone or wooden rams, pestles, and other tools are used to ram the soil layer by layer to make the soil compact and firm. This type of wall is mainly built in areas with soil on the surface, and the distribution range is relatively wide. It is the main method of building the Great Wall.

05

图5　赤城独石口长城全景

Figure 5　Panoramic view of Dushikou Great Wall in Chicheng

　　山势险峻，石筑。

Precipitous mountains, stone constructions

06

图6 赤城独石口长城局部

Figure 6 Part of the Great Wall at Dushikou, Chicheng

  土石混筑墙,是指用泥土和石块混合砌筑的墙体。墙体两侧外壁砌筑石块,内填土或土石夯筑。在长城墙体中,土石混筑墙占有较大比重,主要分布于黄土高原的丘陵地带。

Earth and stone walls refer to walls built with a mixture of soil and stones. The outer walls on both sides of the wall are built with stones, and the inner walls are filled with earth or rammed earth and stone. Among the Great Wall walls, earth-rock concrete walls account for a large proportion and are mainly distributed in the hilly areas of the Loess Plateau.

07

图7　赤城独石口堡长城墙基局部

Figure 7　Part of the base of the Great Wall of Dushikou Fort, Chicheng

　　石砌是从山上采集或从山体上开凿出一定规格的石头，用这些石头垒砌长城，形成的墙体称为石砌墙。

　　形制工整、石材坚实，又称石块砌筑墙，是指通体使用石块砌筑的墙体。石块之间多用黄土或其他黏土黏结，个别石墙外壁用石灰勾缝。这种墙体主要分布于山地。

Stone masonry is stones of a certain size collected or excavated from the mountain, and people use these stones to build the Great Wall, and the former wall is called a stone wall.
The shape is neat and the stone is solid, also known as the stone masonry wall, which refers to the wall made of stone masonry throughout the body. Loess or other clays are often used to bond the stones, and the outer walls of individual stone walls are jointed with lime. This kind of wall is mainly distributed in mountainous areas.

08

图8 赤城独石口堡西南侧墙体
Figure 8 The wall on the southwest side of Dushikou Fort in Chicheng

外层石材垒筑，内部碎石夯填，又称石混筑墙，是指用泥土和石块混合砌筑的墙体，墙体两侧外壁砌筑石块，内填土或土石夯筑。在长城墙体中，土石混筑墙占有较大比重，主要分布于黄土高原的丘陵地带。

The outer layer of stone is built, and the inner crushed stone is rammed and filled, also known as a mixed stone wall, which refers to a wall built with a mixture of soil and stones. The outer wall on both sides of the wall is built with stone blocks, and the inner wall is filled with earth or rammed with earth and stone. Among the walls of the Great Wall, earth-rock mixed walls account for a large proportion, mainly distributed in the hilly areas of the Loess Plateau.

09

图9　赤城独石口长城
Figure 9　Chicheng Dushikou Great Wall

　　峰谷绵延，气势磅礴。
The peaks and valleys are stretching and magnificent.

10

图10 赤城海家窑长城
Figure 10 Chicheng Haijia Kiln Great Wall

敌台，建在长城墙体上，两侧凸出城体，主要用于守城士兵瞭望和防御敌军进攻。碎石垒筑，犹如坚强而忠诚的卫士。

The enemy tower, built on the wall of the Great Wall, protrudes from the city on both sides and is mainly used for guarding soldiers to look out and defend against enemy attacks. Built with gravel, it is like a strong and loyal guard.

11

图11 赤城马连口长城
Figure 11 Maliankou Great Wall in Chicheng

碎石夯层，层叠明显。夯土版筑，则是在墙体宽度的两侧分别埋设成排的木柱或木桩，于木柱或木桩内侧之间铺设横置的木板（版），形成夹板状，然后于两侧木板之间逐层填土、夯实。

Gravel rammed layers with layers obviously. Rammed earth version construction is to bury rows of wooden columns or piles on both sides of the width of the wall, and lay horizontal wooden boards (plates) between the insides of the wooden columns and wooden piles to form a plywood shape. Then, it places them on both sides filling and compacting the side planks layer by layer.

12

图12　赤城盘道界楼匾额
Figure 12　Plaque on the Pandao Boundary Building in Chicheng

　　雄伟的化身。
A majestic symbol.

13

图13 赤城清泉堡北门

Figure 13　North Gate of Qingquan Fort in Chicheng

　　土夹碎石层夯筑，外砌石材和砖，端庄稳固。

The soil was rammed with crushed stone layers, and the exterior was built with stone materials and bricks, which were dignified and stable.

绘话长城

14

图14　赤城清泉堡北门侧面图
Figure 14　Side view of the north gate of Chicheng Qingquan Fort

结构清晰，体现建筑工巧，又称包砖墙或砖包墙，墙体内外两壁为青砖砌筑，内壁填筑夯土或泥土、碎石，是长城砖墙较常见的建造方式。包砖墙主要分布于中国的东部及长城沿线的关隘、山坳及交通沿线的重点防御地段。

The structure reflects the construction skills. It is also called brick-wrapped wall or brick-wrapped wall. The inner and outer walls are made of blue bricks, and the inner wall is filled with rammed stone, mud, and gravel. This is a common construction method for the brick wall of the Great Wall. Brick-clad walls are mainly distributed in eastern China and key defensive areas along passes, mountain passes and transportation along the Great Wall.

绘话长城

15

图15 赤城清泉堡南门敌楼匾额
Figure 15 The plaque on the enemy building at the south gate of Qingquan Fort in Chicheng

永照楼三个字寓意安定。
The three characters of Yongzhao Tower mean stability

16

图16 赤城县上堡村"新添镇川墩"
Figure 16 "Xin Tian Zhen Chuan Pier" in Shangbao Village, Chicheng County

　　这是一个三层敌楼，三层较二层箭窗更小，有矩形箭窗42个。
　　瞭望孔（望口、望孔）设在长城墙体顶部垛口上部的小孔多呈正方形，主要用于守城士兵观察、瞭望敌情。

This is a three-story watch tower, and the third floor has smaller arrow windows than the second floor with 42 rectangular arrow windows.
Lookout hole (lookout, lookout hole) is a small hole located on the top of the crenellation on the top of the Great Wall. It is mostly square and mainly used for soldiers guarding the city to observe and look out for the enemy.

17

图17　赤城松树堡城门楼

Figure 17　The gate tower of Chicheng Pine Castle

18

图18 赤城长城
Figure 18 Chicheng Great Wall

  垒筑长城用的石材多为含铁矿石。

  石墙用石块砌筑的墙体，根据建造方式的不同又分为毛石干垒墙、土石混筑墙、石块砌筑墙等几种类型。

Most of the stone materials used to build the Great Wall are iron-containing ores.

The stone wall is a wall made of stones. According to different construction methods, they are divided into several types such as rubble dry walls, earth and stone concrete walls, stone masonry walls, etc.

图19 赤城长沟门坝头长城
Figure 19 Chicheng Changgoumenbatou Great Wall

画卷徐徐展开·赤城

20

图20　赤城长伸地堡镇虏楼匾额
Figure 20　Plaque of Changshen Bunker Town Lu Building

21

图21 赤城长伸地堡镇虏楼

Figure 21　Lu Building of Chicheng Changshen Bunker Town

　　砖砌空心敌台，建筑形制端庄高大，楼体四个方向建有券形箭窗。楼体内部有券室、券道，券室或券道内筑有梯道，砖砌阶梯，直通台顶，台顶有垛口。

The hollow lookout tower is built of bricks, and the building is dignified and tall, there are arch-shaped arrow windows in the four directions of the building. There are arch rooms and arch paths inside the building. Stairways are built in the arch rooms or arch channels, and brick stairs lead directly to the top of the platform which has crenels.

22

图22 赤城长伸地堡旗杆基石
Figure 22　Flagpole Cornerstone of Chicheng Changshen Bunker

外圆内方，呈现出机械感。
The outer circle and the inner square present a mechanical sense.

图23　赤城镇安堡长城
Figure 23　Anbao Great Wall in Chicheng Town

这是利用山险采用黄土夯筑长城墙体构成的防御性工事。

　　山险是借助或直接利用崖壁、沟壑、险峻的山势、高耸的山脊等作为天然屏障，与长城墙体共同构成的防御性工事。主要分布于山区，无人为加工痕迹，是古人利用自然地形、地势、地物的巧思创造。

It is a defensive fortification composed of the Great Wall walls made of loess rammed by taking advantage of the mountain risks.
The dangerous mountains rely on cliffs or directly draw support from cliffs, ravines, steep mountains, towering ridges, etc. as natural barriers and defensive fortifications formed together with the Great Wall walls. Mainly distributed in mountainous areas, there are no traces of human processing. It is an ingenious creation of the ancients using natural topography, topography, and features.

绘话长城

24

图24　崇礼
Figure 24　Chongli

25

图25 赤城和崇礼交界的马连口长城局部
Figure 25　Part of the Maliankou Great Wall at the Junction of Chicheng and Chongli

　　实心敌楼外壁砌筑石块，内部填充碎石。

　　实心敌台平面呈正方形，外壁砌筑石块或砖，内部填充土石等，台体一侧多建有登台的阶梯式步道，顶部四周或建垛口，垛口上置瞭望孔，底部设排水口。

The outer wall of the solid watch tower is built of stones, and the interior is filled with gravel.
The solid enemy platform is square in plane, with the outer wall made from stones or bricks, and the interior filled with earth and stone. There are often stepped walkways on one side of the platform, and crenelations may be built around the top with observation holes on the crenels and a drainage outlet on the bottom.

绘话长城

26

图26　赤城和崇礼交界的马连口长城全景
Figure 26　Panoramic View of the Maliankou Great Wall at the Junction of Chicheng and Chongli

因地势起伏构筑，视野辽阔，联动防护。

山险墙是在自然山险的基础上经人为加工形成的防御性工事。山险墙均分布于山脉连绵起伏的山区，主要修建在山势险峻处，有明显的人为加工痕迹。

Due to the undulating terrain, it has a wide field of vision and linkage protection.

The mountain wall is a defensive fortification formed by artificial processing based on the natural mountain risks. The mountain walls are all distributed in the rolling mountainous areas. They are mainly built in steep mountains and have obvious traces of human processing.

图27　崇礼清三营乡长城
Figure 27　The Great Wall of Qingsanying Township in Chongli

烽燧，又称墩台、烽堠、烟墩、狼烟台、狼烟墩，汉代称烽堠、亭燧、亭堠等，唐代以后称烽火台，明代称烟墩或墩台，是建在长城沿线或交通要道沿线、建于山顶或易于观察和瞭望之处，用以点燃烟火传递报警信息的高台。它作为报警及传递信息的设施，是长城防御系统的重要组成部分。在长城的相关建筑及设施中，烽燧的功能与作用是最重要的。夜间点火，称为烽；白天燃烟，称为燧。

Beacon Towers, also known as Pier, Beacon, Smoke Pier, Wolf Smoke Platform, Wolf Smoke Pier, etc. In the Han Dynasty, it was called Fenghou, Tingsui, Tinghou, etc. After the Tang Dynasty, it was called the Feng Fire Platform. In the Ming Dynasty, it was called Yandun or Pier Platform. They were built on the Great Wall along the line or the traffic arteries, which were built on the top of the mountain or observe and look out easily. The high platform is used to ignite fireworks to transmit alarm information. As an alarm and information transmission facility, it is an important part of the Great Wall defense system. Then, among the related buildings and facilities of the Great Wall, the function of fire beacon towers is the most important. Lighting a fire at night is called Feng and burning smoke during the day is called explosion.

28

图28 沽源
Figure 28 Guyuan

29

图29 沽源盘道沟长城
Figure 29　Pandao Trench Great Wall in Guyuan

　　砖砌实心敌楼，有券形门洞下方两侧置挂石，用于悬挂软梯，攀爬痕迹清晰。
The solid watchtower is built of bricks with hanging stones on both sides below the coupon-shaped door opening, which is used to hang soft ladders. And the climbing traces are clear.

30

图30　沽源和赤城交界的长城

Figure 30　The Great Wall at the Junction of Guyuan and Chicheng

高险兼备的敌台与碎石垒筑的梯形墙体共同形成守护屏障。

The high-risk lookout tower and the trapezoidal wall built with gravel jointly serve as a protective barrier.

31

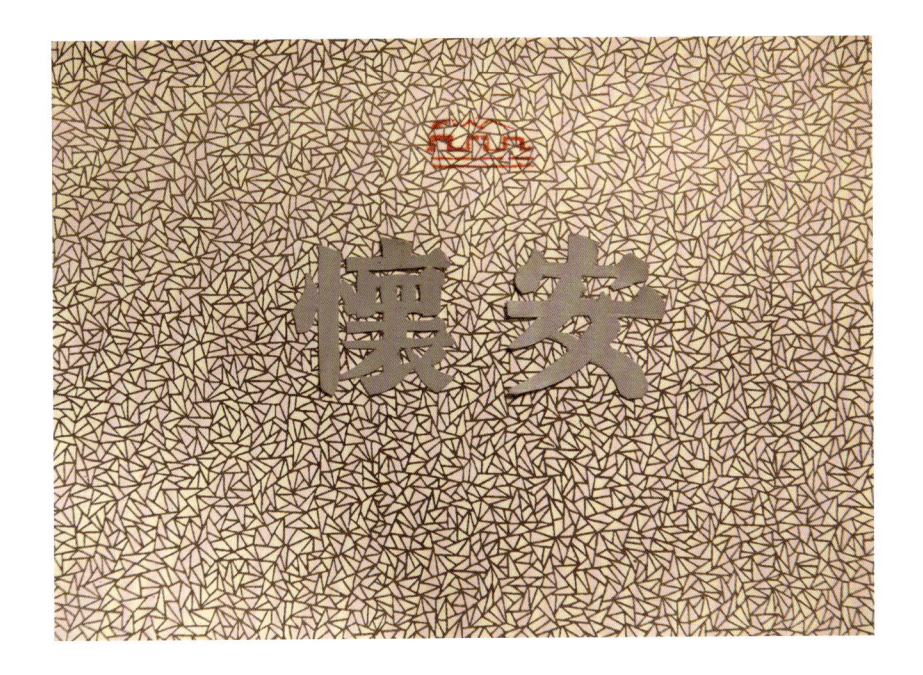

图31　怀安
Figure 31　Huaian

图32　怀安渡口堡西门

Figure 32　West Gate of Huaian Ferry Fort

内部夯土，外层砖砌，形制规整。

包砖墙，又称砖包墙。墙体内外两壁为青砖砌筑，内壁填筑夯土或泥土、碎石，是长城砖墙较常见的建造方式。包砖墙主要分布于中国的东部及长城沿线的关隘、山坳及交通沿线的重点防御地段。

The interior is of rammed earth, the exterior is of brick, and the shape is regular.
Pack brick wall, is also known as brick-cover wall. The inner and outer walls of the wall are made of blue bricks, and the inner wall is filled with rammed earth, soil, and gravel. This is a common construction method of the Great Wall brick wall. Brick-clad walls are mainly distributed in eastern China and key defensive areas along passes, mountain passes and transportation along the Great Wall.

33

图33 怀安马市口长城
Figure 33 Huaian Mashikou Great Wall

  二十号敌台，空心敌台为石基砖身，具有烽火台和敌台的双重功能，距地面约3.7米处嵌有一块方形石匾，刻着"得胜台"字样以及建造的时间。

No. 20 lookout tower, the hollow lookout tower is a stone-based brick body, which has the dual functions of a beacon tower and a lookout tower. A square stone plaque is embedded about 3.7 meters above the ground, engraved with "Victory Tower" and the time of construction.

画卷徐徐展开·怀安

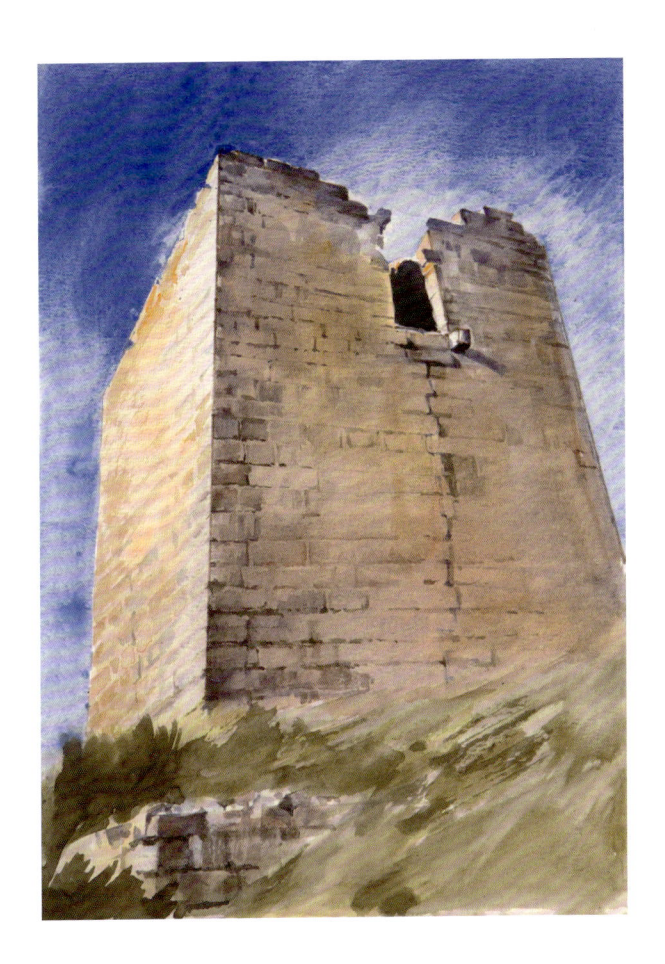

34

图34 怀安桃平盘道门长城敌楼

Figure 34　The enemy building of the Great Wall at Pandaomen, Taoping, Huaian

　　石砌的实心敌楼可以看到利用绳索攀岩的痕迹。

A solid watchtower built of stone， you can see the traces of rope climbing.

085

图35　怀来
Figure 35　Huailai

36

图36 怀来水头长城
Figure 36 Shuitou Great Wall in Huailai

　　圆形敌楼碉堡，环山建构碉堡，将箭窗与通道贯通为一体，与依山崖峭壁砌筑的石墙相连，易守难攻，彰显建造智慧。

The circular watchtower blockhouse, built around the mountain, connects the arrow window with the passage, and the stone wall is built on the cliff, which is easy to defend, also it is difficult to attack, demonstrating the wisdom of construction.

图37 怀来水头长城圆形敌楼马面全景

Figure 37 Panoramic view of the circular watchtower and horse face of Shuitou Great Wall in Huailai

以仰视的角度记录这段有代表性的长城，山脊沟壑的险峻与建造的防御工事巧妙衔接。

　　马面，又称城垛、墙台、墙垛，平面多呈正方形，也有圆形。凸出墙体外侧，与长城墙体等高，台体为夯土筑造或外壁砌筑砖石，实心。通常建在重要的关隘、处于交通要道附近地势较平缓地带的长城墙体上，主要用于守城士兵从侧面或两翼夹击攻城的敌兵。

Record this section of the Great Wall from the perspective of looking up. The precipitousness of the ridges and gullies is ingeniously connected with the fortifications built.

Horse faces, also known as battlements, wall platforms, and wall stacks, are mostly square in plane, and sometimes round in plane. It protrudes from the outside of the wall and is as high as the wall of the Great Wall. The platform body is built of rammed earth, or the outer wall is built of masonry with solid. It is usually built on the wall of the Great Wall in an important pass or on a relatively gentle terrain near the main traffic road. It is mainly used for the defenders to attack the enemy soldiers attacking the city from the side or two wings.

图38 怀来陈家堡长城

Figure 38　Huailai Chenjia Fort Great Wall

长城与山势起伏融汇贴合，犹如山的筋脉，体现出明代长城的恢宏壮观。

这段长城建筑规格高，条石砌筑规整，城基、高度和顶宽各个部分比例严谨，排水檐、泄水孔、垛口、墙台等配套设施科学，作为样边推广。

样边，样：样板、示范。边：边墙、长城。为了保证长城修筑的质量，选择部分地段按照标准修建样板工程，供其他修筑长城的人参观学习。

The Great Wall and the ups and downs of the mountain blend, just like the tendons of the mountain, reflecting the magnificence of the Great Wall in the Ming Dynasty.

This section of the Great Wall has high architectural specifications, regular stone masonry, strict proportions of city foundation, height and top width, and scientific supporting facilities such as drainage eaves, scupper holes, crenels, and wall platforms, which are promoted as samples.

Sample size, sample is model, demonstration. The side is side wall, the Great Wall. To ensure the quality of the construction of the Great Wall, some areas were selected to build model projects according to the standards for other people who built the Great Wall to visit and learn.

39

图39 怀来陈家堡将军楼

Figure 39 Huailai Chenjia Fort General Building

  按照箭窗的多少来命名，敌楼防御墙面上有三个箭窗称"三眼楼"；有四个箭窗称"四眼楼"。将军楼有六个箭窗，因此又称"六眼楼"，它是一个二层敌楼，内部有对窗和对门的隔墙，以通道相连，当地人又称"三街六巷楼"。建筑形制严谨规整，是陈家堡长城保存最为完整的大型敌楼。

According to the number of arrow windows, there are three arrow windows on the defensive wall of the watch tower, which are called "three-eye building"; there are four arrow windows, which are called "four-eye building". The general building has six arrow windows, so it is also called a "six-eye building". The architectural shape is rigorous and regular. It is the most complete large-scale watch tower in the Chenjia Fort Great Wall.

40

图40 怀来陈家堡长城由双砖结构砌成

Figure 40 The Chenjia Fort Great Wall in Huailai is built with a double-brick structure

  以画笔描绘砖石砌筑结构的时候为工程细节所感动。

  砖石混砌墙，是指以条石为基础，上部用青砖砌筑两侧墙壁，内部填筑夯土或泥土、碎石的墙体。砖石混砌墙在长城各种墙体中最为坚固，但耗费人力、物力，成本高，因此主要分布于明长城沿线一些重点防御地段。

I was inspired by the engineering details when drawing the masonry structure with a brush.
Brick-and-stone concrete wall refers to a wall that is based on strips of stone, with blue bricks on both sides of the upper portion, and the interior is filled with rammed earth, soil, or gravel. Brick and stone concrete walls are the strongest among the various walls of the Great Wall, but they consume a lot of manpower, and material resources, and are costly. Therefore, they are mainly distributed in some key defensive areas along the Great Wall in the Ming Dynasty.

41

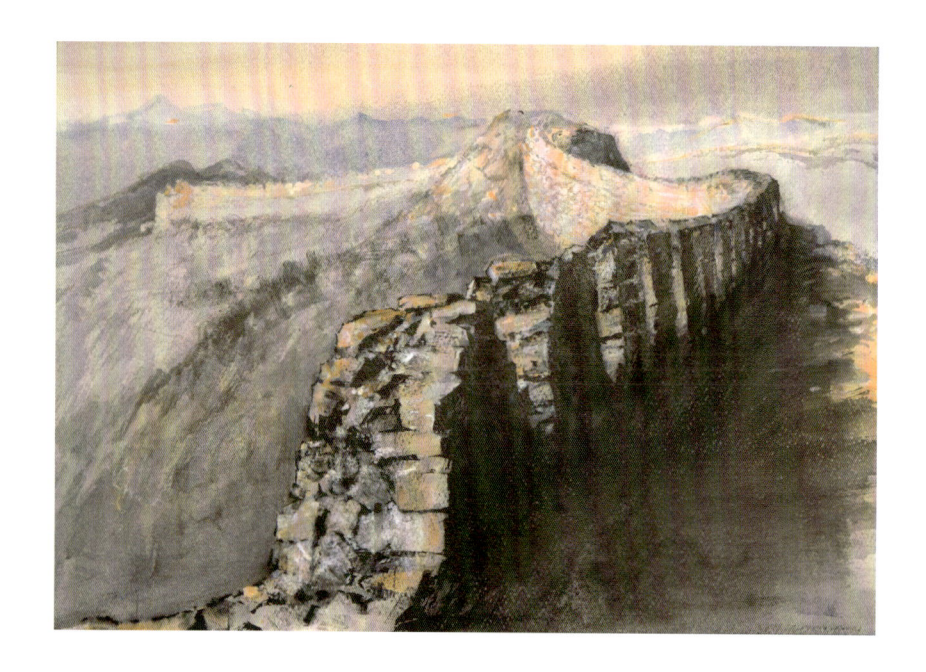

图41 怀来大营盘
Figure 41 Huailai Dayingpan

垛口（女口、雉堞、垛口墙），即长城墙体顶部呈连续凹凸矩形缺口状的矮墙，多建在长城墙体顶部的外侧，有些地段墙体顶部两侧均建垛口。垛口的底部一般呈向外斜坡状，主要用于瞭望远处敌情，也可做向较远处或探身向下射箭之用。

Crenel (Nvkou, Zhidie, crenel wall) The top of the Great Wall is a low wall with a continuous concave-convex rectangular notch shape. Most of them are built on the outside of the top of the Great Wall. In some areas, crenels are built on both sides of the top of the wall. The bottom of the crenel is generally in the shape of an outward slope, which is mainly used to look out for the enemy's situation in the distance. It can also be used to shoot arrows farther away or leaning down.

42

图42　怀来鸡鸣山驿匾额

Figure 42　The Plaque of Jiming Mountain Station in Huailai

驿道是中国古代重要的交通通道，主要用于运送物资、传递军情信息。长城沿线多分布有驿道及驿站，为长城防卫提供便利。

Post Road was an important transportation channel in ancient China, mainly used to transport materials and transmit military information. There are many post roads and post stations scattered along the Great Wall which provide convenience for the defense of the Great Wall.

图43 怀来鸡鸣驿城墙
Figure 43 The City Wall of Jiming Station in Huailai

  青砖砌垒内夯黄土，墙高15米。
  砖墙长城内外两壁外观是以砖砌为主的墙体。因使用材料和建造方式不同，砖墙又分为包砖墙、砖石混砌墙两种类型。

The loess is rammed inside the blue brick base, and the wall is 15 meters high.
The inner and outer brick walls of the Great Wall are mainly made of bricks. Due to different materials and construction methods, brick walls are divided into two types brick-clad walls and masonry-concrete walls.

44

图44 怀来罗锅长城

Figure 44　Huailai Luoguo Great Wall

  此处长城蜿蜒曲折，90°的折弯迂回，70°坡起高低落差。

  女墙（又称宇墙、女垣、女儿墙），长城墙体顶上高约一米的矮墙，多建在墙体内侧，有射孔，可以起到拦护和对抗防守攻城敌军的作用。

Here the Great Wall twists and turns with 90-degree bends circuitous turns, and 70-degree slopes with height differences.

Nvqiang (also known as Yuqiang, Nvyuan, and Parapet) is a low wall about one meter high on the top of the Great Wall. It is mostly built on the inside of the wall and has perforations. It serves to block and resist the enemy siege as a defensive role.

45

图45　怀来罗锅长城箭孔

Figure 45　Arrow Holes in Huailai Hunchback Great Wall

　　箭孔又称射孔，是建在长城墙体顶部垛口下部或障墙上的小口，主要用于守城士兵用弩射杀敌兵。箭孔形状以长方形、顶部呈圆拱形为主，还有一些多边形，如图。

Arrow holes, also known as perforations, are small openings built on the lower part of the crenels at the top of the Great Wall or on the barrier wall. They are mainly used by soldiers defending the city to shoot and kill enemy soldiers with crossbows. The shape of the arrow hole is mainly rectangular with a round arch at the top, and some polygons, as shown in the illustration.

46

图46 怀来石洞3号敌台

Figure 46　Enemy Tower No. 3 in Huailai Stone Cave

　　因画面左上部分的现存形态形状像五根手指而被称为五指楼。

Because the existing form in the upper left part of the picture is shaped like five fingers, it is called the Five Finger Building.

47

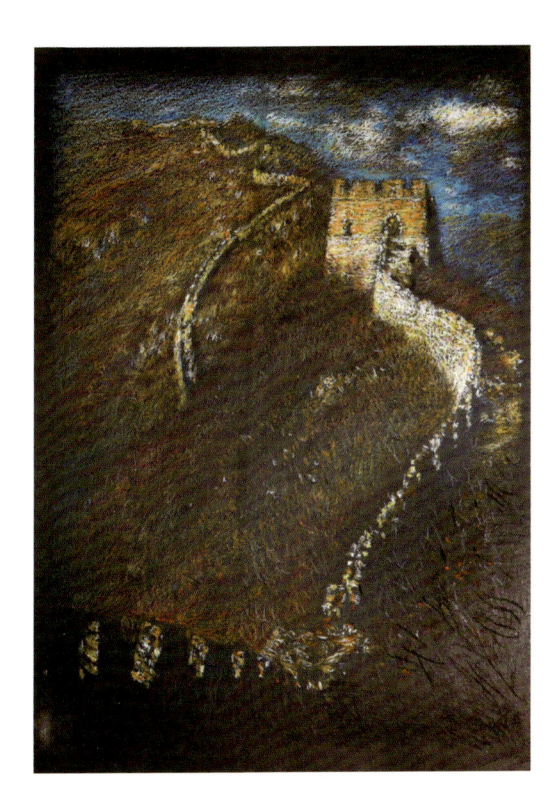

图47　怀来水头长城
Figure 47   Huailai Water Head Great Wall

　　毛石干垒墙、毛石是指自然形成、未经人工分拣的石头，石块之间不用泥土黏结。这类墙体主要建造在石质的山地上。

Rough stone drywall and rough stone refer to stones that are naturally formed and have not been sorted by humans. Rough stone drywall refers to a wall made of large hand stones stacked and built. Between the stones, there is no need to stick with the soil. This type of wall is mainly built on stone mountainous terrain.

图48 怀来样边长城供士兵上下城墙的台阶

Figure 48 The steps of the Great Wall in Huailaiyang for soldiers to go up and down the wall

  登城步道建在长城墙体内侧的阶梯多呈台阶状，主要用于士兵上下城墙。这些附建在长城墙体上的设施均具有加强长城防御、有效阻止敌方进攻以及保护长城本体的作用。

The climbing trail is built on the inner side of the Great Wall. It has a step shape and is mainly used for soldiers to go up and down the city wall. These facilities attached to the Great Wall have the function of strengthening the defense of the Great Wall, effectively preventing enemy attacks, and protecting the Great Wall itself.

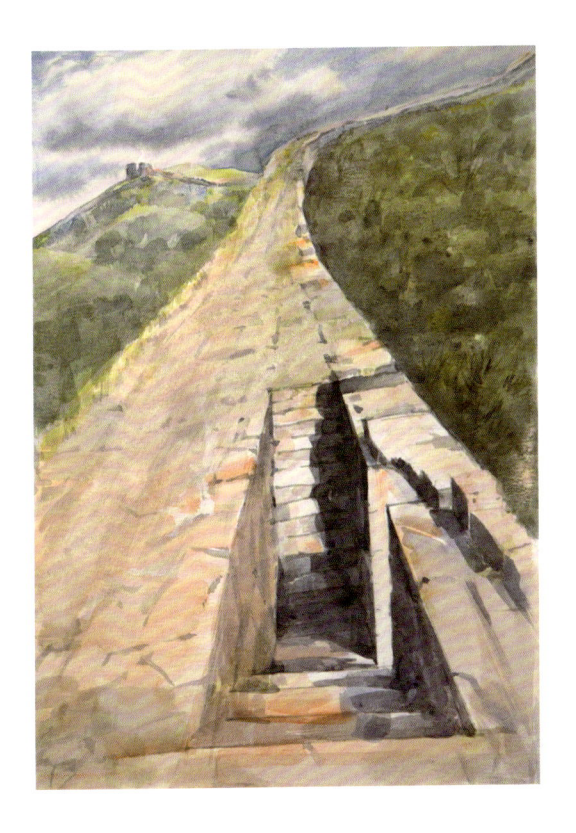

图49 怀来样边长城内侧每200米一个门洞，有台阶供上下

Figure 49 Inside the Great Wall in Huailaiyang Edge Great Wall, there is a doorway with steps going up and down every 200 meters.

50

图50 怀来样边长城水门特写

Figure 50 Close-up of the Water Gate of the Yangbian Great Wall in Huailai

　　水门，在长城关险中还有一类配套设施称水门，或称长城跨越山涧、河谷或河流时，在长城墙体下部修建的门洞，主要是供流水穿过长城，避免因水流，特别是山洪造成对长城培体的冲击和破坏。在枯水季也是交通便道，具有供人马通行的功能。在水门上方的长城墙体修建有城楼等建筑，又称水关。

Water gate, in the Great Wall Pass, there is another kind of supporting facility called a water gate, or when the Great Wall crosses mountains, valleys, or rivers, the door openings built in the lower part of the Great Wall walls are mainly for water to pass through the Great Wall to avoid water flow. It was the flash flood that caused the impulsiveness and destruction of the Great Wall. In the dry season, it is also a traffic access road, which has the function of passing people and horses. There are towers and other buildings built on the wall of the Great Wall above the water gate, also known as the Watergate.

图51 怀来样边长城水门样式
Figure 51　Watergate Style of the Great Wall in Huailai Yangbian

　　排水口为排泄长城墙体底部的积水，在城墙内侧底部修筑的排水沟和排水口均建在长城墙体相对较低的地段。由此排水口外接石质排水槽。

The drainage outlet is used to drain the accumulated water in the body of the Great Wall. The drainage ditches and drainage outlets built at the bottom of the inner side of the wall are all built in relatively low areas of the Great Wall. There is an external stone drainage channel connected to this drainage outlet.

52

图52　康保
Figure 52 Kangbao

53

图53 康保金界壕1
Figure 53 Kangbao Jinjiehao1

壕堑（亦称壕沟、界壕） 采用挖境沟、堆土筑墙的方式建造而成，是由壕沟、壕体共同组成的防御性工事，主要分布于平原地带。

A trench (also known as a trench and boundary trench) is constructed by digging trenches and piling earth to build walls. It is a defensive fortification composed of trenches and trench bodies. It is mainly distributed in plain areas.

54

图54　康保金界壕2
Figure 54　Kangbao Jinjiehao 2

　　堆土墙，即在地表直接堆土成墙，不经夯实，因此墙体内部结构比较松散，墙体前面呈弧形。这类墙主要分布在黄土地带，多为早期长城的建造方式。
Piles of earth walls are piles of the earth directly on the surface to form a wall without compaction. Therefore, the internal structure of the wall is relatively loose and the front of the wall is curved. This type of wall is mainly distributed in loess areas and is mostly built in the same way as the early Great Wall.

55

图55　尚义
Figure 55　Shangyi

56

图56　尚义地上村（西赵家窑）长城
Figure 56　The Great Wall of Dishang Village (West Zhaojia Kiln) in Shangyi

57

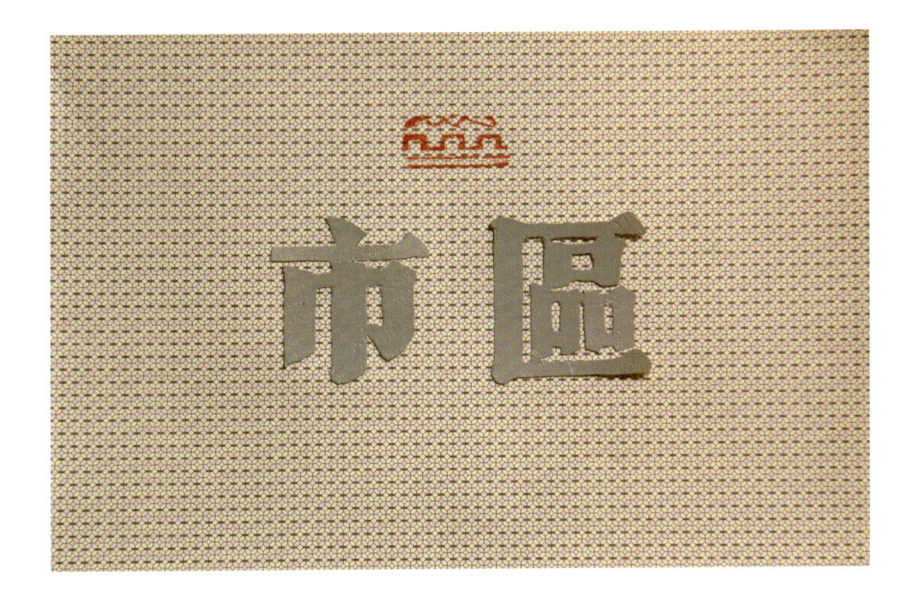

图57 市区

Figure 57 Shiqu

图58　堡子里文昌阁
Figure 58　Wenchang Pavilion in Baozi

城障是在长城险要处修筑的供官兵驻守的小城，一般只在一面设门，四角有斜出的墙台。长城沿线这类建筑一般面积较大，设施齐备，多建有城墙、护城壕、城门、城楼、角楼或角台等，墙体外侧建有马面，顶部外侧筑有垛口，具有较强的防御功能。城内有衙署、兵营、仓储及民居、街道、庙宇、水井等基本分区，有些城堡内外附近还建有烽火台以及陶窑等辅助设施。作为长城重要后援的城堡，也有一些兼作府、州、县的治所，或扼守交通枢纽，兼作交通要道沿线的驻兵之地。这些城堡多分布于长城内侧沿线的交通要道及交通枢纽地区，与长城本体之间或有烽火台相联系，或有驿道等道路相连接。

A city barrier is a small city built at a dangerous location on the Great Wall for officers and soldiers to garrison. It usually only has a gate on one side and sloping wall platforms at the four corners. Such buildings along the Great Wall generally have large areas and complete facilities. They often have city walls, moats, gates, towers, turrets or turrets, etc. There are horse faces on the outside of the wall and crenels on the outside of the top, which have a strong sense of security for defense function. The city is divided into basic divisions such as government offices, barracks, warehouses and residences, streets, temples, and wells. Some castles also have beacon towers, pottery kilns, and other auxiliary facilities nearby. As an important backup for the Great Wall, some castles also served as the administrative offices of prefectures, prefectures, and counties, guarded transportation hubs, and served as garrison locations along major transportation routes. These castles are mostly located in the traffic arteries and transportation hub areas along the inner side of the Great Wall. They may be connected to the Great Wall itself by beacon towers or by roads such as post roads.

59

图59　桥东区威远台
Figure 59　Weiyuan Terrace, Qiaodong District

图60　桥西区东窑子镇墩台
Figure 60　Qiaoxi Dongyaozi Town Beacon Tower

　　敌台（敌楼、墩台）　建在长城墙体上，两侧凸出城体，主要用于守城士兵瞭望和防御敌军进攻。多建在位于地势较开阔或较高地段的长城墙体上，敌台有实心、空心两种形制。

Lookout towers (watch towers and piers) are built on the wall of the Great Wall, with protrusions from the city on both sides. They are mainly used for the defenders to watch and defend against enemy attacks. They are mostly built on the walls of the Great Wall located in relatively open or higher areas. The lookout towers come in two shapes, solid and hollow.

61

图61　市区石匠窑长城

Figure 61　Mason Kiln Great Wall in Shiqu

挡马墙又称羊马垣、副墙、小长城，是建在长城本体外，与长城墙体或护城壕相连的墙体。挡马墙是针对北方游牧民族善骑射的特点而采用的一种有效的阻击方式，即将战马阻挡在距长城本体一定的距离外，使骑兵优势难以发挥，有助于增强长城防御的功能。

The horse-retaining wall, also known as the Yangma Wall, the auxiliary wall, and the small Great Wall, is built outside the Great Wall itself and connected to the Great Wall walls or moat. The horse-retaining wall is adopted in response to the characteristics of the northern nomadic people who are good at riding and shooting. An effective blocking method blocks the war horses at a certain distance from the Great Wall itself to make it difficult for the cavalry to take advantage of it and help to enhance the defense function of the Great Wall.

画卷徐徐展开 · 市区

62

图62　市区石匠窑至菜市村长城

Figure 62　From Shijiang Kiln to Caishi Village Great Wall in Shiqu

63

图63 西镜门
Figure 63 Xijing Gate

  关隘又称关口。或分别称为关、口，是指长城墙体上的通道口。多建在长城沿线重要的交通要道上，一般由关门、关城组成。

  关城作为关口的屯兵之所，是关险重要的配套设施，由城墙、城门、城楼、角楼构成，属于城保性质。

  关门既是出入长城内外的通道，也是防御的重点。故关门外侧多建有瓮城，为关口增添了一道防线。

Pass is also called the strategic pass known as pass or gateway, and it refers to the passageway opening on the wall of the Great Wall. Most of them are built on important traffic arteries along the Great Wall. It is generally composed of city gate and fort.

The fort serves as a garrison station at the pass. It is an important supporting facility for the city security. It consists of city walls, city gates, city towers, and turrets of a city security nature.

The city gate is not only the passage to and from the Great Wall but also the focus of defense. Therefore, there are many barbicans outside of the gate, which adds a line of defense to the gate.

64

图64　万全

Figure 64　Wanquan

65

图65　教堂楼两角度

Figure 65　Two Angles of the Church Building

多层砖堆砌平整，使得整个垛墙十分坚固，抵御外围土石地面挤压以及人为破坏与风蚀。

造型准确，色彩对比明显，画面和谐又给人静谧的感觉。

Multiple layers of bricks are stacked evenly, making the entire stacked wall very strong and resistant to the extrusion of the surrounding earth and stone ground, as well as man-made damage and wind erosion.

The shape is accurate, the color contrast is obvious, and the picture looks harmonious and gives people a sense of tranquility.

66

图66　万全教堂楼
Figure 66　Wanquan Church Building

断壁残垣之中，原始城墙与孔洞历经风霜岁月，依旧傲然挺立。

整体画面主次分明，用笔松弛有度，虚实结合恰到好处，细节刻画很醒目，虽然楼梯残破，但仍显得坚固挺拔。

Among the ruins, the original city walls and holes still stand proudly despite the years.
The overall picture has clear priorities, the pen is relaxed and moderate, and the combination of the virtual and the real is just right. Then, the details are very eye-catching. Although the stairs are broken, they appear strong and straight.

67

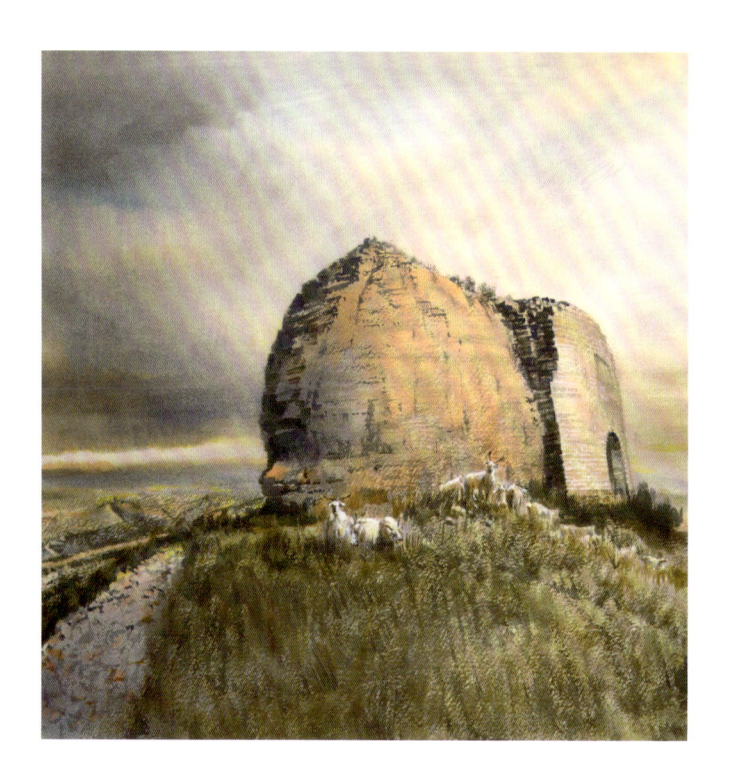

图67　万全威远东空台1

Figure 67　Wanquan Weiyuan East Air Station 1

　　曲面城门口，展开环形城墙砖块堆积。

　　画面平静，几只羊羔的点缀为整体增添了乐趣，生动又自然。

At the curved city gate, bricks are piled up in a circular city wall.
The picture is calm, and the embellishment of a few lambs adds fun to the whole vivid and natural.

68

图68 万全威远东空台2
Figure 68 Wanquan Weiyuan East Air Station 2

筒形城门口，多层砖石挤压与聚集，使得整体稳固向内聚拢贴合。
At the cylindrical city gate, multiple layers of masonry are squeezed and gathered, making the whole structure stable and concentrically gathered together.

69

图69　万全西孤山

Figure 69　Wanquan West Gu Mountain

不规则砖石沿山体绵延竖起一层坚固屏障。

画面错落有致，墙壁造型灵动，石块的排布有韵律感。

Irregular masonry stretches along the mountain to erect a thick solid barrier.
The pictures are well-proportioned, the shapes of the walls are flexible, and the arrangement of stones has a sense of rhythm.

图70 万全洗马林倒V字墙

Figure 70 Wanquan Xima Forest inverted V-shaped wall

沿山体交错竖起两个方向的屏障。

意象清远，一望无际，墙壁向远处延伸，能深切体会山的绵延。

Barriers in two directions were erected along the mountain.
Imagery is clear and distant, stretching as far as the eye can see. The walls extend into the distance, and you can deeply appreciate the stretching of the mountains.

71

图71　万全洗马林长城席家窑段

Figure 71　Wanquan Xima Forest Great Wall Xijia Kiln Section

　　蜿蜒曲折的山脊上筑起长蛇般的坚固砖石围墙。
　　画面层次丰富，颇有苍凉的意境。

A solid brick and stone wall that looks like a snake was built on the winding ridge. The picture is rich in layers and has a rather desolate artistic conception.

画卷徐徐展开·蔚县

72

图72　蔚县
Figure 72　Yu County

127

73

图73 蔚县单堠堡关帝庙
Figure 73 Guandi Temple in Danyu Fort, Yu County

蔚县单堠村关帝庙正门两侧的两个石表，当地人称"石"，圆杆方斗结合了"表"和"杆"的形态，从顶部依次为宝珠、葫芦、素面圆杆、小斗、雕龙圆柱、大斗、有垂莲浮雕的圆柱、柱础。

融合了硬山顶墙体与悬山顶墙体以及塔形杆体（表体），独具特色与符号辨识度。

光感很强烈，点、线、面运用得淋漓尽致，画面动静结合，主次分明，鸟群的动感与建筑的静止，让人仿佛身临其境，时间仿佛被拉长了。

The two stone tables on both sides of the main entrance of Guandi Temple in Danhou Village, Yu County. Local people call them stones. The round poles and square buckets combine the shapes of "tables" and "poles". From the top, they are orbs, gourds, plain round poles, small buckets, dragon-carved columns, big buckets, columns with hanging lotus reliefs, and column bases.

It combines the hard top wall, the cantilever top wall, and the tower-shaped pole body (surface body) with unique characteristics and symbolic recognition.

The sense of light is very strong, and dots, lines, and planes are used vividly. The picture combines dynamic and still with clear priorities. The movement of the birds and the stillness of the building make people feel as if they are on the scene, and time seems to have been stretched.

74

图74 蔚县单堠村关帝庙东石表柱础顶部雕覆莲，腰部雕琴、棋

Figure 74 The top of the east stone pillar base of the Guandi Temple in Danhou Village, Yu County is carved with a lotus covering the top, and the waist is carved with piano and chess pieces.

标识性极强的石表对称地坐落在房屋前方作为进出此地区的独特标识与纪念雕刻碑。

The highly iconic stone table is symmetrically located in front of the house as a unique sign and commemorative sculpture for entering and exiting the area.

75

图75　蔚县单堠村关帝庙西石表柱础顶部雕覆莲，腰部雕书、画

Figure 75　The top of the west stone column base is carved with lotus coverings. The waist of the west tower is carved with calligraphy and paintings.

　　柱础方正，上面圆柱居中，多层次展现雕刻技巧与花纹。

The column base is square, and the upper column is centered, showing carving techniques and patterns on multiple levels.

76

图76　蔚县单堠村村外有堡壕，黄土夯筑的堡围墙

Figure 76　There is a fort outside Danhou Village in Yu County, and a fort wall made of rammed loess.

不同方向的城墙走势由中间延伸至外围，边缘高低错落，增加宽度防御力。

罗城是关城在城墙外侧加建的一些小城圈，多呈凸出状。城墙外侧还挖有护城壕，关城内建有衙署、兵营、仓储、民居、店铺等，有些关城附近还建有场、互市等交易场所，供长城内外的物资交流。

河险借助陡峭的河岸、宽深湍急的河水，或两山之间狭窄的河道作为天然屏障，无人为加工痕迹，但容易受水情不稳、河道变迁的影响。

The city walls in different directions extend from the middle to the outer edge, and they are staggered at different heights to increase the width and defense.

Luo City is a fort with some small city circles added on the outside of the city wall, most of which are in the shape of protrusions. There are also city protection structures dug outside the city wall. There are government offices, military barracks, warehouses, residences, shops, etc. built in fort. Some forts also have markets, mutual markets, and other trading places nearby to facilitate the exchange of materials inside and outside the Great Wall.

River risks using steep river banks, wide, deep, and fast rivers, or narrow river channels between two mountains as natural barriers. There are no traces of human processing, but they are easily affected by unstable water conditions and changes in river channels.

77

图77　蔚县单堠村堡门1

Figure 77　The stone round arch gate in Danhou Village, Yu County 1

圆拱门提供给 人车良好的进出可达性和加固墙体两侧的贴合度和稳定性。

色彩对比强烈，结构准确，画面中心细节丰富，整体呈现一种淡雅古朴的感觉。

The round arch provides good accessibility for people and vehicles and reinforces the tightness and stability of both sides of the wall.

The color contrast is strong. The structure is accurate. The center of the picture is rich in details, and the overall feeling is elegant and simple.

图78 蔚县单堠村堡门2
Figure 78 The stone round arch gate in Danhou Village, Yu County 2

　　出于防卫需要在大门内有插木质门闩的石制栓眼，垒砌在石材和夯土结构中，合理地利用砖块接缝角落将门部件镶嵌进砖墙中。
For defense purposes, there is a stone eyelet with a wooden latch in the door. Built into a stone and rammed earth structure. Reasonable use of brick joint corners to embed door components into the brick wall.

图79 蔚县单堠村内街巷

Figure 79 Streets and lanes in Danhou Village, Yu County

融合平房顶和硬山瓦顶及朴素的灰白砖石墙房屋。

线条流畅，干湿浓淡，相得益彰，虚实结合得恰到好处。

驿站又称递铺、驿馆、驿递，是专为长城防御体系设置的供传递文书，来往官兵中途住宿、补给、换马的处所，建在与长城相连的交通要道上。因其功能主要是满足过往官兵住宿的基本需求，一般规模有限，主要有围墙、大门、居住的房屋、马厩、水井等建筑及设施。

Houses that blend bungalows with pediment roofs with gray and white masonry plain walls.

The lines are smooth. The dry and wet shades complement each other, and the combination of the virtual and the real is just right.

Post stations, also known as delivery stores, post houses, and post stations, were specially designed for the Great Wall defense system to deliver documents and provide accommodation, supplies, and horse exchanges for officers and soldiers. They were all built on the main transportation routes connected to the Great Wall. Because its function mainly meets the basic needs of accommodation for passing officers and soldiers. It is generally limited in scale and mainly includes buildings and facilities such as walls, gates, residential houses, stables, and wells.

图80 蔚县古堡
Figure 80　Yuxian Castle

　　夯土土堡连接道路与房屋。
　　画面中红色的灯笼艳而不俗，仿佛点亮了整个古朴的画面，生活气息浓郁，作者生动且真实地表达了当地人民对生活的热爱。

Rammed earth-colored earth forts connect roads and houses.
The red lanterns in the picture are bright and elegant seeming to light up the entire simple picture. The atmosphere is rich in life. The author expresses the local people's love for life vividly and truly.

画卷徐徐展开·蔚县

81

图81　蔚县古堡影壁

Figure 81　Yuxian Castle Screen Wall

　　影壁突出在房屋前遮挡风沙，具有文化、习俗及缓冲气流影响的多重意义。整体画面静谧，色彩和谐。

The screen wall protrudes in front of the house to block the wind and sand and has multiple expressive meanings of form, climate influence, and customs.
The overall picture is quiet, and the colors are harmonious.

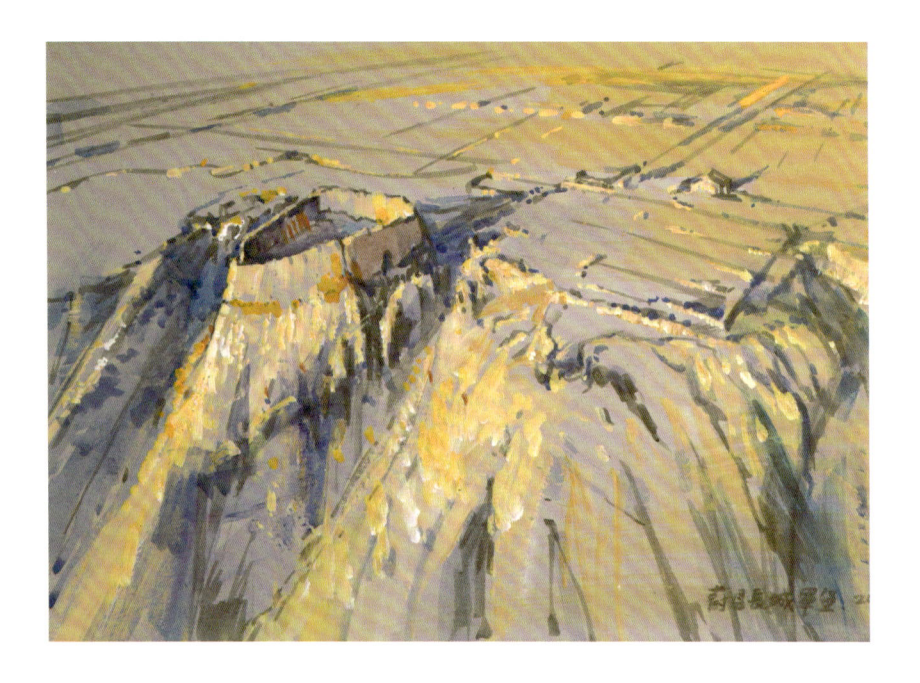

图82 蔚县西大坪军堡
Figure 82 Xidaping Military Fort in Yu County

此军用堡垒坐落于陡峭山岭上，四周多高低错落起伏，利于孤守与观察四周多方向变化。

　　线条纵横交错，节奏感强，作者用笔干净利落，刚柔并济，整体造型神形兼备。

　　有一类属于城堡性质的建在长城本体及烽火台附近，或驿道、交通要道沿线的小城堡，亦称边堡、军堡、屯堡等，主要为戍守长城及烽火台、驿道士兵的驻守之所。这类城堡的主要功能是屯驻。所以面积均不大，建筑设施相对较简单，一般由城墙（或称堡墙）、城门（或称堡门）及城内的住所组成，少数城堡建有角楼或角台，城墙外侧挖有护城壕，具有一定的防御功能，城内建有供士兵居住的房屋，间数或多或少，亦有成排的房屋建筑，还有水井、磨坊、庙宇等配套制式。

This military fortress is located on a steep mountain with many undulating heights around it to make it easy to stand alone and observe changes in the surrounding directions.

The lines are crisscrossed and have a strong sense of rhythm. The author's brushwork is clean and neat with a combination of hardness and softness. And the overall shape is both spiritual and physical.

There is also a type of small castles that are built near the Great Wall and beacon towers, or along post roads and traffic arteries. They are also called border forts, military forts, and forts. They are mainly built to guard the Great Wall, beacon towers, and post roads. The place offered soldiers staying. The main function of this type of castle is to maintain residence. Therefore, the area is not large, and the construction facilities are relatively simple. They are generally composed of a city wall (or fort wall), a city gate (or fort gate), and residences in the city. A few forts have turrets, and protective guards are dug outside the city walls. The city has a certain defensive function. There are houses for soldiers to live in, with more or less rooms. There are also rows of buildings, as well as wells, mills, temples, and other supporting facilities.

83

图83 蔚县羊圈堡军堡

Figure 83 Yuxian Sheep Pen Castle Military Residence

此军堡墙体自然形成羊圈堡封闭性屏障,利于区隔四周与中心平地区域。

色彩明亮、丰富且统一,整体构图生动有趣,层次丰富,近景远景错落有致,细节刻画很出彩。

住所又称居住地,是戍守长城或烽火台士兵的住所。一般建在长城墙体、堑等长城本体附近。多为一所房屋,面积不大。

The wall of this military residence naturally forms a closed barrier for the sheepfold Castle, which helps to separate the surrounding and central flat areas.

The colors are bright, rich, and unified, the overall composition is lively and interesting, rich in layers, the close-up and distant views are well-proportioned, and the details are brilliant.

Residence, also known as living place is the residence of soldiers guarding the Great Wall or Beacon Tower. They are generally built near the Great Wall body such as walls and trenches. Most of them are one house with a small area.

84

图84　宣化
Figure 84　Xuanhua

85

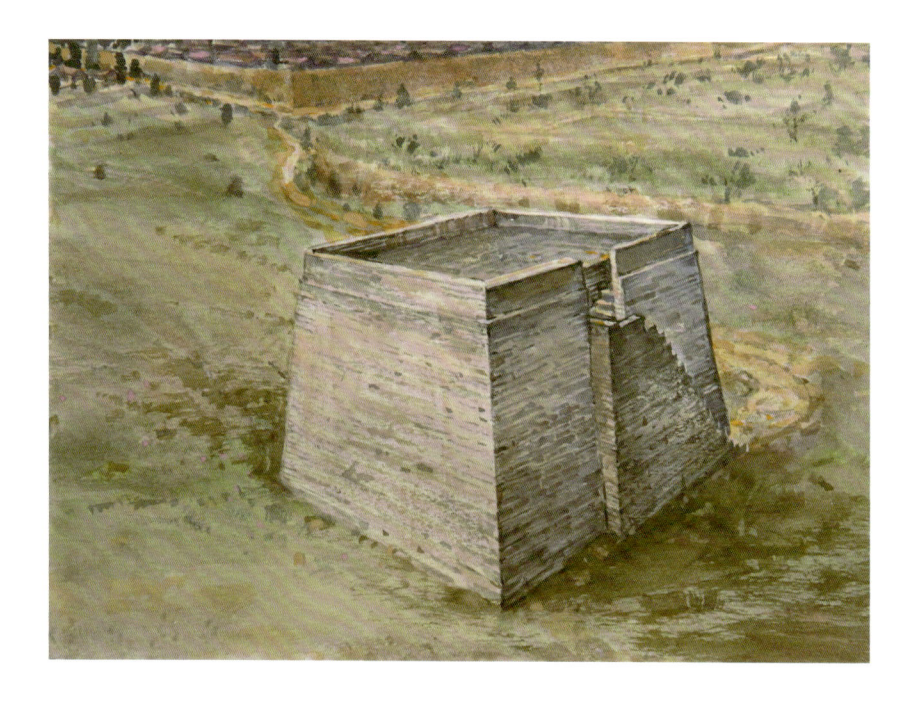

图85 宣化东望山乡葛峪堡点将台

Figure 85 Geyu Fort Dianjiang Terrace, Dongwangshan Township, Xuanhua

高耸的四方垛墙，稳固的上小下大墙体形立面平实结实，坐落于平地区域，十分突出，易于观察与部署周围环境。

The towering square stacked walls, the stable upper small walls, and the lower large wall-shaped facades are flat and solid. It is located in a flat area and is very prominent, making it easy to observe and arrange the surrounding environment.

画卷徐徐展开·宣化

86

图86 宣化凤凰山长城（石墙）

Figure 86 Xuanhua Phoenix Mountain Great Wall (Stone Wall)

绵延冗长的城墙依山而建，蔓延山脊区隔两侧山面。

笔触相对大胆强烈，对造型结构进行了很好的归纳。构图主次分明，长城的局部和整体都得到了体现。

The long city wall is built against the mountain, and the spreading ridge separates the mountains on both sides.
The brush strokes are relatively bold and strong, and the shape structure is well summarized. The composition has clear priorities, and both parts and the whole of the Great Wall are reflected.

87

图87　宣化后坝村空心敌楼

Figure 87　Hollow Watchtower in Houba Village, Xuanhua

　　高耸的敌楼利于观察周围态势并提供四方可达性，以及防御出其不意的多方来敌。
　　刻画对象体积浑厚，采用自下而上的视角，运笔描绘富有层次变化。

The high watch tower is conducive to observing the surrounding situation, providing accessibility from all directions, and providing unexpected defense against enemies coming from many directions.
The objects depicted are large and thick, using a bottom-up perspective, and the brush strokes are full of layered changes.

图88 宣化青边口长城敌楼
Figure 88 Xuanhua Qingbiankou Great Wall Watchtower

独立高耸的四方敌楼有着光滑的砖体墙面和平整的楼顶，便于快速观察与防御阻挡四周山中敌人靠近。

采用俯视的视角，主体造型写实，透视准确，整体画面色彩丰富统一。

The independent and four-sided tall watch tower has smooth brick walls and a flat roof, which facilitates quick observation and defense to block the approach of enemies in the surrounding mountains.

Adopting an overhead perspective, the main body shape is realistic. The perspective is accurate, and the overall picture is rich and unified in color.

89

图89 宣化青边口长城空心敌台挂绳梯处
Figure 89 Xuanhua Qingbiankou Great Wall Hollow Enemy Platform Hanging Ladder

绳梯处紧密地嵌在箭窗，便于观察周边环境以及快速操作绳梯部件和收纳物品，既坚固又实用。

主体结构清晰，造型准确，色彩对比强烈，画面虚实结合，突出主体。

The rope ladder is tightly embedded in the arrow window, making it easy to observe the surrounding environment and quickly operate the rope ladder components and store items. It is both sturdy and practical.

The main body structure is clear, the shape is accurate. The color contrast is strong. The picture combines virtuality and reality to highlight the main body.

90

图90　宣化青边口挂绳梯处细部图

Figure 90　Detailed View of the Rope Ladder at Qingbiankou, Xuanhua

从箭窗内俯视挂绳梯处，石质部件与墙体紧密贴合、牢固，距离适宜。明暗对比强烈，结构清晰精准，色彩丰富。

Looking down at the rope ladder from the arrow window the stone parts fit closely and the wall making it suitable to secure the distance.
The contrast between light and dark is strong. The structure is clear and precise, and the colors are rich.

图91　宣化青边口长城
Figure 91　Xuanhua Qingbiankou Great Wall

　　沿山脊纵向分割山势两侧，竖起曲折垂直的墙体，而且良好地平衡两侧重力，使得整体稳固平实，使碎石堆叠的长城宛若游龙守护着这片山岗。

　　画面构图富有动感，错落有致，通过色彩设计，使主体明确，笔触大胆强烈，给人自由灵动的感觉。

Zigzag vertical walls are erected on both sides of the mountain along the ridge longitudinally. And the gravity on both sides is well-balanced to make the whole structure stable and level. The Great Wall, stacked with rubble, is like a wandering dragon guarding this hill。

The composition of the picture is dynamic and well-proportioned. Through the color design, the subject is clear, and the brushstrokes are bold and strong giving people a feeling of freedom and flexibility.

92

图92　阳原
Figure 92　Yangyuan

93

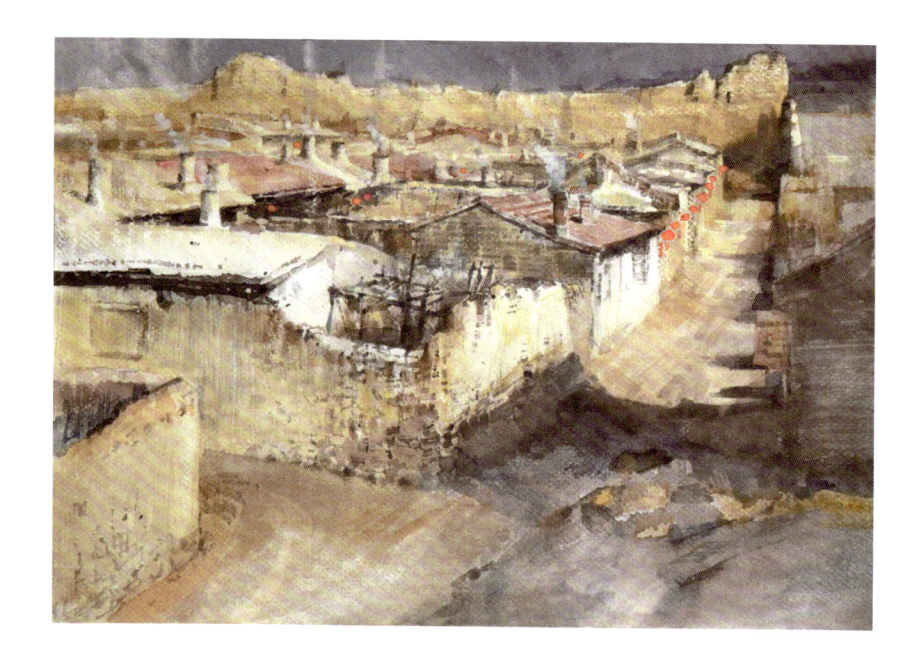

图93　阳原开阳古堡1
Figure 93　Yangyuan Kaiyang Castle 1

俯瞰城内古堡分布均匀和谐，外围墙体半包围聚合多排房屋。

　　全景布局，点、线、面运用灵活，细节刻画到位，红色的灯笼和烟囱里的烟虽只占画面的一小部分，但却使整个画面生机勃勃。

　　夯土墙，夯土是指在堆土时使用夯或杵进行夯砸、压实，其中又有堆土夯筑、版筑两种类型。堆土夯筑，是在堆土时逐层使用石质或木质的夯、杵等工具，反复、细密地夯砸，以使土质紧密、牢固。夯土版筑，则是在墙体宽度的两侧分别埋设成排的木柱或木桩，在木柱或木桩内侧之间铺设横置的木板（版），形成夹板状，然后在两侧木板之间逐层填土、夯实。这类墙体主要建在地表为土质的地带，分布范围比较广，是长城建造的主要方式。

Overlooking the city, the castles are evenly and harmoniously distributed. The outer walls are semi-encircled by multiple rows of houses.

Panoramic layout, and flexible use of points, lines, and surfaces are well-depicted details. Although the red lanterns and smoke from the chimney only occupy a small part of the picture, they make the picture full of vitality.

Rammed earth wall, rammed earth refers to the use of rams or pestles for tamping and compaction mounding soil. There are two types of earth mound construction and block construction. Compounding soil means using tools such as stone or wooden rammers and pestles to ram soil layer by layer repeatedly and finely to make the soil compact and firm. Rammed earth board building is to burying rows of wooden columns or wooden piles on both sides of the width of the wall, and lay horizontal wooden boards (boards) between the insides of the wooden columns or wooden piles to form a plywood shape, and then place them on both sides. Filling and compacting soil layer by layer between the side planks. This type of wall is mainly built in areas with soil on the surface. It is also distributed over a wide range. It is the main method of constructing the Great Wall.

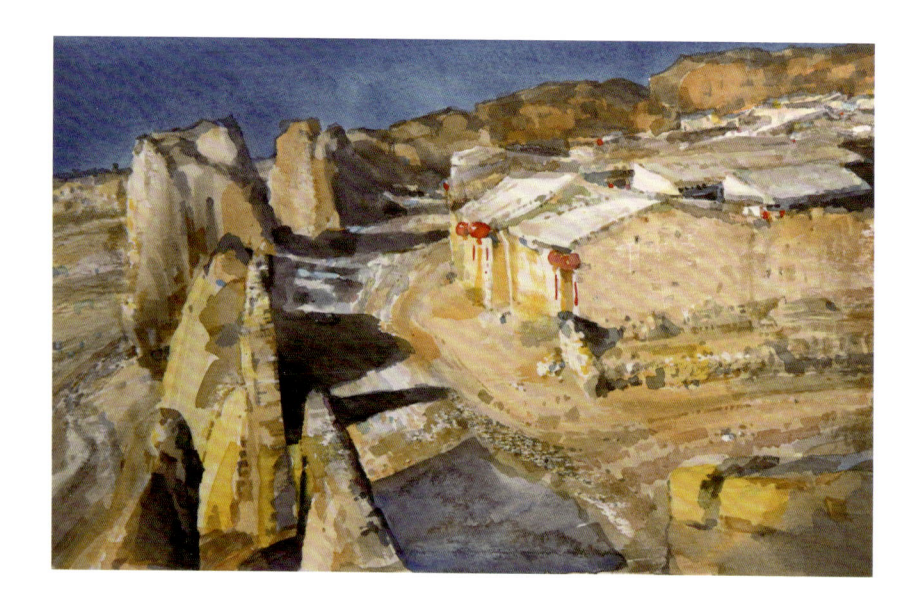

图94 阳原开阳古堡2
Figure 94 Yangyuan Kaiyang Castle 2

　　单层房屋聚落外围由高低错落的坚固夯土墙遮挡防护，做到内外区也遮挡风沙及防御人为威胁。

　　色彩对比强烈，光感十足，红色作为点缀十分亮眼。画面的延展性很强，空间感十足。

The outer perimeter of the single-story house settlement is shielded and protected by solid rammed earth walls of varying heights so that both the inner and outer areas are shielded from wind, sand, and defend against man-made threats.
The color contrast is strong. The light is full, and the red is very eye-catching as an embellishment. The picture is very malleable and has a full sense of space.

95

图95 阳原开阳古堡门
Figure 95 Yangyuan Kaiyang Castle Gate

  厚砖石墙门口与崎岖路面构成城门垛墙的底部。
  运用一点透视,指引观众的目光,细节刻画到位。
  城堡又称城障、障城、镇城、障塞、塞,为筑有城墙的指挥、驻兵之所。

The thick masonry wall entrance and rugged road surface construct the bottom of the city gate's battlements.
Using a one-point perspective to guide the audience's gaze and depicting details in place.
A castle is also called a city barrier, barrier city, town city, barrier fort, or fortress. It is a commanding place and garrison place with walls.

96

图96 阳原开阳古堡门匾额
Figure 96 Plaque on Kaiyang Castle Gate in Yangyuan

雕刻的门匾牢固地镶嵌在墙体上。
The carved door plaque is firmly embedded in the wall.

97

图97　阳原马圈堡

Figure 97　Yangyuan Maquan Fort

　　由周围夯土与砖石共同组建的墙体紧密地连接，高低错落地满足不同用途的人防与马圈的目的，合理地利用地势和分区。

　　以暖色调为主，画面明亮，中心几棵树线条生动，"破"开以大面积色块为主的画面，让整幅作品有了呼吸，绿色在暖色中的点缀也带来生命力。

The walls composed of surrounding rammed earth and masonry are closely connected and staggered at different heights to meet the purpose of civil defense for different purposes while making reasonable use of terrain and zoning.

The painting is dominated by warm colors, and the picture is bright. The lines of the trees in the center are vivid, which "breaks" the picture dominated by large areas of color and allows the whole work to breathe. The embellishment of green in the warm colors also brings vitality.

98

图98　张北
Figure 98　Zhangbei

画卷徐徐展开·张北

99

图99 张北野狐岭

Figure 99　Zhangbei Wild Fox Ridge

一望蜿蜒坚固的夯土墙体与山上土地和谐地融合。

色彩和谐统一，暖黄色与熟褐色的结合，不禁让人想起米勒的画面，也联想到熟悉又温暖的故乡田野。

At first glance, the wriggling solid rammed earth wall blends with the land on the mountain harmoniously.

The colors are harmonious and unified. The combination of warm yellow and ripe brown helps people remember Miller's paintings and the familiar warm fields of his hometown.

100

图100 张北正边台长城

Figure 100 Zhangbei Zhengbian Terrace Great Wall

山岭上长城矗立着，仿佛自然地从山丘中长出的笔直连绵的竖墙。
整体画面给人一种苍茫辽阔的感觉。

The Great Wall stands on the mountain ridge as if it is a straight and continuous vertical wall growing naturally from the hills.
The overall picture gives people a sense of vastness.

101

图101　涿鹿
Figure 101　Zhuolu

图102 涿鹿白家口敌台内景

Figure 102 Interior view of Baijiakou Enemy Tower in Zhuolu

砖石堆砌的牢固十字交叉拱券型垛墙门口与顶部，内外空间连接顺畅紧密，光线充分进入便于多角度观察环境。

　　线条流畅，用笔刚劲，结构明确，整体风格写实。

The solid cross arch-shaped stacked wall door and top made of bricks and stones provide a smooth and tight connection between the internal and external spaces. And, the light fully enters to facilitate observation of the environment from multiple angles.
It has the feel of smooth lines, firm brushwork, a clear structure, and a realistic overall style.

图103　涿鹿白家口西门上方匾额

Figure 103　The plaque above the west gate of Baijiakou, Zhuolu

便于识别的匾额有着雕刻的花纹和方正字镶嵌在砖石墙身中。

The easily identifiable plaque has carved patterns and square characters embedded in the masonry wall.

104

图104 涿鹿白家口壹号敌台箭窗

Figure 104 Arrow Window of No. 1 Enemy Platform at Baijiakou, Zhuolu

箭窗和射口牢固紧密地镶嵌于砖石砌筑的垛墙中,便于观察和防护外来攻击。

The arrow window and the nozzle are firmly and tightly embedded in the masonry stacked walls to facilitate observation and internal protection from external attacks.

图105 涿鹿白家口龙字贰号敌台礌石孔

Figure 105　Lei Stone Hole on No. 2 Longzi Platform, Baijiakou, Zhuolu

使用三角形的城砖砌筑垛口边缘的立墙，充分扩大守城者的视野和防守面。垛口旁圆形射口在墙中开阔视野，便于观察和利用，光滑平实的墙面砖石组合与统一营造稳固的堡垒顶部。

　　礌石孔长城垛口墙底部的孔洞多成双成对，建在位于山口或山谷间的长城墙体上。通过礌石孔用绳索拴绑吊筐或滚木、圆形的石头用于守城士兵在城墙上掷滚木、礌石，砸攻城的敌人。

Using triangular city bricks for the construction of vertical walls at the edge of crenels to fully expand the defender's field of vision and defensive area. The circular opening is next to the crenel widely field of view in the wall for easy observation and utilization. The smooth and flat masonry wall combination and unity create a stable top of the fortress.

The holes at the bottom of the crenelated walls of the Great Wall are mostly in pairs and built on the Great Wall located at the mountain pass or between the valleys. A hanging basket or a rolling log is tied with a rope through the stone hole, and a net-shaped stone is placed inside the hanging food container. It is used to put lacquer and stone in the upper box of the Temple City Plan to defend the city. It is an effective way to play the role of destroying the enemy by dropping stones.

106

图106　涿鹿白家口龙字伍号敌台匾额

Figure 106　No. 5 Tai Plaque with Dragon Character in Baijiakou, Zhuolu

形制规整，字体方正，雕刻于砖石墙体中。

主体造型严谨，明暗对比强烈，富有体积感。

The regular and square fonts are carved into the masonry walls.

The main body shape is rigorous with strong contrast between light and dark, and a sense of volume.

107

图107 涿鹿白家口龙字伍号敌台回廊
Figure 107 Corridor of the Look-out Tower No. 5, Longzi, Baijiakou, Zhuolu

沿着垛墙内长廊，多个箭窗、射口与门连接提供丰富的外界光线和视野，以及稳固的厚墙防御，利于内部穿插、移动和多角度观察。

Along the inner corridor of the corrugated walls, multiple arrow windows, nozzles, and doors are connected to provide abundant external light and views, as well as solid thick wall defense, which facilitates internal penetration, movement, and multi-angle observation.

108

图108　涿鹿白家口龙字伍号敌台中心室拱券与储物室
Figure 108　The arch and storage room in the central room of No. 5 Longzi Look-out Tower in Baijiakou, Zhuolu

纵横交错的拱门由墙体链接，分隔成多个高矮不一的空间，用于储存和人流动等不同目的。

铺舍（楼橹、铺房），是建在墙体顶部或敌台上的建筑物，多为一间或数间房屋，主要供守城士兵躲避风雨，也是士卒临时休息和储备军用物品的场所。

The crisscrossing arches are connected by walls and divided into multiple spaces of different heights for different purposes such as storage and people flow.
Pushe (Loulu, bun house) is a building built on the top of the wall or the lookout tower. It is mostly one or several houses. It is mainly used for the soldiers guarding the city to take shelter from wind and rain. It is also a place for the soldiers to rest temporarily and store military supplies.

绘话长城

109

图109 涿鹿白家口龙字陆号敌台
Figure 109　Zhuolu Baijiakou No. 6 Longzi Enemy Tower

　　垛墙中门与墙体闭合完整，区隔空间，易使用。

The door in the stacked wall is completely closed with the wall making the separated space which is easy to use.

110

图110 涿鹿白家口龙字陆号敌台滚石口

Figure 110 Zhuolu Baijiakou No. 6 Longzi Enemy Tower Rolling Stone Entrance

多个垛口和高低错落的射口提供多角度与高度的视野，便于观察和防御马道周围和两侧环境、敌人等的变化。

Multiple crenels and staggered nozzles provide a wide range of angles and heights of vision, making it easy to observe and defend against changes in the environment, personnel, enemies, etc. around and on both sides of the horse track.

图111 涿鹿白家口龙字敌台内台阶

Figure 111　The Steps Inside the Dragon-shaped Look-out Tower in Baijiakou, Zhuolu

缩小窄砖石楼梯节省空间，便于加固及单人快速稳定地移动或防御。

The narrow masonry staircases save space, facilitate reinforcement and allow a single person to move or defend quickly and stably.

图112 涿鹿龙字叁号敌台上旗杆石和水嘴
Figure 112　Flagpole Stone and Water Spout on No. 3 Enemy Platform, Zhuolu Longzi

　　排水系统部件牢固结实地与城墙融合，旗杆各部件保存良好，易制作，合理稳固。
　　虚实结合，主体物准确，整体画面丰富，笔触自然有力。

The drainage system components are firmly integrated with the city wall, and the flagpole components are well preserved, easy to make and reasonably stable.
The virtual and real are combined, and the subject is accurate. The overall picture is rich, and the brushstrokes are natural and powerful.

图113 涿鹿马水口叁号敌台内部结构图

Figure 113 Internal Structure Diagram of the No. 3 Lookout Tower at Mashuikou, Zhuolu

　　垛墙内长廊狭窄紧密，多个门、箭窗交错分布于两边，便于周围不同角度和方向的观察并防御外部。

　　画面视觉冲击感强烈，结合明亮的色彩，把光感描绘得淋漓尽致，富有美感。

The corridor inside the crenellated wall is narrow and tight with multiple doors and arrow windows staggered on both sides to facilitate observation and defense of the outside from different angles and directions.

The picture has a strong visual impact, combined with bright colors, and vividly depicts the sense of light full of beauty.

图114　涿鹿马水口捌号敌台

Figure 114　No. 8 Look-out Tower at Mashuikou, Zhuolu

马道宽度、箭窗和垛墙门口尺度与人、马等尺度和谐，便于移动和观察防御，并且马道高度和垛墙高度连接紧密，合理地分隔山两侧。

　　马道或是建在长城墙体内侧，供人马通行的道路，或是建在长城墙体顶部的通道。其中建在墙体内侧的马道多呈斜坡状，亦有阶梯状，主要用于向长城墙体顶部运送物资及供守城士兵行走。

The width of the horse path, the arrow window, and the scale of the crenelated wall entrance are harmonious with the scales of people and horses which makes it easy to move, use, and observe defense. The height of the horse path and the height of the crenelated wall are closely connecting and dividing the two sides of the mountain reasonably.

Horse paths are either built on the inside of the Great Wall for people and horses to pass through, or they are built on the top of the Great Wall. The horse paths are built on the inside of the wall with the shape of slopes or steps. They are mainly used to transport supplies to the top of the Great Wall and the soldiers who defend the city to walk.

115

图115 涿鹿马字拾号台匾额

Figure 115 Ma Zi Number Ten Station Plaque of Zhuolu

便于识别的匾额有着雕刻的花纹和方正字镶嵌在砖石墙身中。

The easily identifiable plaque has carved patterns and square characters embedded in the masonry wall.

116

图116 涿鹿马水口敌台条石基座与砖相接的四角石立柱载横卧条石与箭窗相接

Figure 116　The stone base of the lookout tower at Mashuikou in Zhuolu is connected with the bricks. The four cornerstone pillars carry horizontal stones. And they are connected with the arrow window.

　　条石基座上方的垛墙自然地被挑高，便于垛墙内俯视观察外部环境，从内部门口由上到下可做攻击态势，便于防御及合理地利用箭窗和高度。
　　色彩柔和，整体画面稳定，线条流畅明确，细节丰富。

The stacked wall above the stone base is naturally elevated to overlook the external environment from the stacked wall easily. The attacking postures are from top to bottom, from the internal doorway defense easily, with rational use of arrow windows and height.
The colors are soft, and the overall picture is stable. The lines are smooth and clear, and the details are rich.

图117 涿鹿马水口长城残存的箭窗
Figure 117　The Remaining Arrow Window of the Mashikou Great Wall in Zhuolu

圆拱门尺度合理稳固，便于倚靠和观察防御，垛墙之间马道清晰、高耸、坚固。蜿蜒曲折的马道连接多个垛墙使其整体统一，十分坚固实用，高耸陡峭地均匀分隔两侧山体。

The size of the round arch is reasonable and stable, which makes it easy to lean on and observe defenses. The horse path between the stacked walls is clear, tall, and solid. The zigzag bridleway connects multiple stacked walls to make it unified as a whole. They are very strong and easy to use. Also, the tall and steep mountains on both sides are evenly divided.

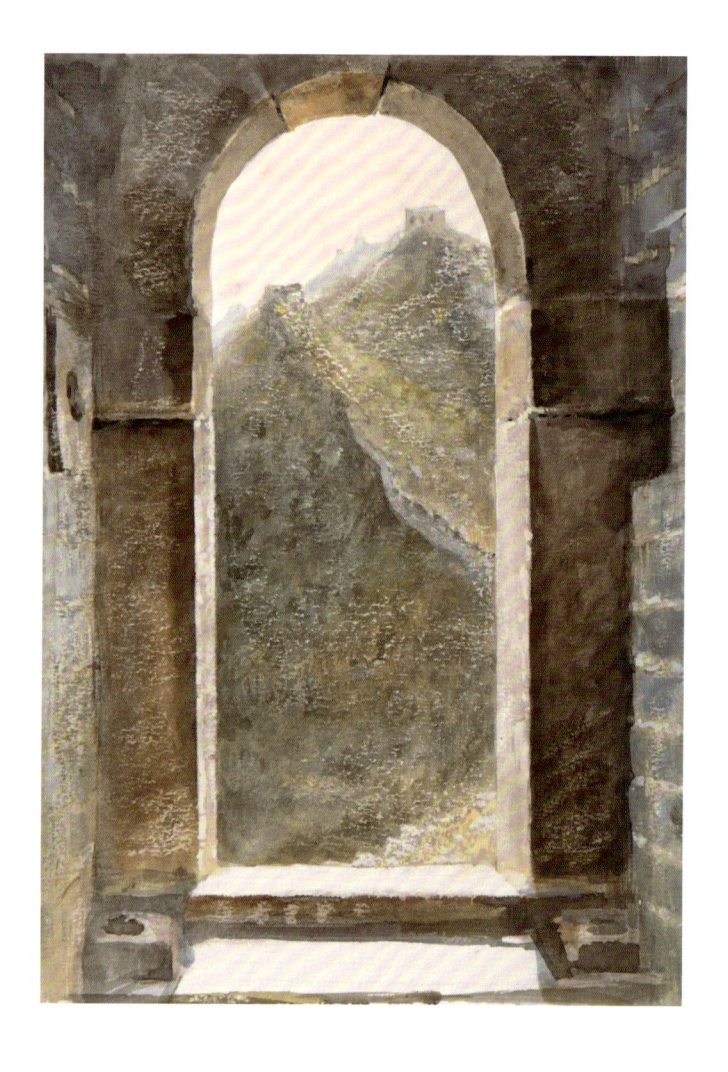

图118　涿鹿水头长城

Figure 118　Zhuolu Shuitou Great Wall

关隘又称关口，或分别称为关、口，是指长城墙体上的通道口。多建在长城沿线重要的交通要道上，一般由关门、关城组成。

　　色彩丰富且统一，着色浓淡、干湿并用，通过笔触将墙面的斑驳体现出来。

Pass (Guanai) is also called the gateway, also known as pass or gateway, it refers to the entrance opening on the wall of the Great Wall. Most of them are built on important traffic arteries along the Great Wall. It is generally composed of city gate and fort.

The colors are rich and unified using both dry and wet ink shades, and the mottled texture of the wall is revealed through brush strokes.

长城主题创作

The Great Wall Theme Creation

长城主题创作

119

图119 《长城之上》被河北美术馆收藏
Figure 119 *Above the Great Wall* was collected by the Hebei Art Museum

图120 《长城脚下》
Figure 120 *At the foot of the Great Wall*

长城主题创作

121

图121 《璀璨生辉》被河北省政府收藏
Figure 121　*Brilliant* was collected by the Government of Hebei Province

绘话长城

后记
Postscript

行走在张家口市14个县市的古堡和长城古遗址中，尝试着以油画、水粉、水彩等材料和技法表现长城的不同形态、结构和肌理，更像是从各个维度与长城对话。画面诉说着一个又一个话题，慢慢感悟到长城不仅仅是建筑，更是一种独特的符号语言，不断地向世人传递着时间长河中每一个节点的信息。与这种信息建立起沟通能够转化为一股力量，每一次都能激发出新的创作构思，并融入日常的创作中。曾经长城之上是响亮的号角，今日长城脚下是无尽的欢乐，每个人都在长城凝聚成的精神力量中成长。

谨以此书致敬历代长城的建造者和保护者。
书写长城、绘画长城的责任担当必将继续。

Walking among the ancient castles and ancient ruins of the Great Wall in 14 counties and cities in Zhangjiakou City, I tried to express the different shapes, structures, and textures of the Great Wall by using various materials and techniques such as oil painting, gouache, and watercolor. This was more like having a dialogue with the Great Wall from all perspectives. The pictures told one topic and another, and I gradually realized that the Great Wall is not only a building and all related facilities, but also a unique symbolic language that continuously conveys information to the world with every node of the long river of the time. In the meanwhile, establishing communication with this kind of information can turn into a kind of force that can inspire new creative ideas every time and integrate them into daily creation. There used to be loud horns on the Great Wall, but today is full of endless joy at the foot of the Great Wall. Everyone grows in the condensed spiritual culture of the Great Wall.
This book is dedicated to the memory of all generations of the Great Wall builders and protectors.
The responsibility of writing and painting the Great Wall will continue.